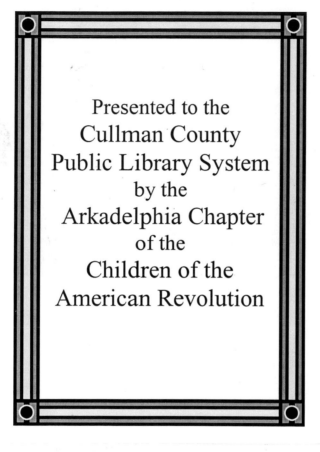

Presented to the
Cullman County
Public Library System
by the
Arkadelphia Chapter
of the
Children of the
American Revolution

CENTENNIAL
PLUS ONE

CENTENNIAL PLUS ONE

*The Centennial History
of the National Society
of the Children of the
American Revolution*

1895–1996

By Eleanor Smallwood Niebell

1895   1995

C.A.R. Press
Washington, D.C.

This Book is Dedicated To

HARRIETT MULFORD LOTHROP

Founder and First President

1895–1901

ACKNOWLEDGMENTS

The author wishes to express her thanks
for the assistance of :

Patricia Love Stephens
Senior National President 1994-1996

Mrs. Charla Borchers Leon
Senior Special Events Chairman 1994-1996

Mrs. May Day Taylor
Consulting, Advertising and Research Services, Inc.

and

Mrs. Joseph Wathen
Administrator, N.S.C.A.R.

TABLE OF CONTENTS

PREFACE

Little did I realize that when Patricia Love Stephens, Senior National President (1994-1996), asked me to become her Printing Chairman in 1994, that I was beginning a journey that would lead to the publication of the official history of the first century of the National Society of the Children of the American Revolution. It has been a task which I can truly report to have been a labor of love.

Centennial Plus One was written to provide members and future members with the complete history of the N.S.C.A.R. from 1895 through 1996. Although several articles had been written about the organization, this is the only book to cover the complete history in detail. As a society dedicated to the history of the United States, it is imperative that we understand and preserve our own history as well as that of the nation.

I have included pictures of National Presidents, Junior National Presidents, and Senior National Presidents in chronological order; details of the organizations development; photographs of important or interesting events; many of the accomplishments of members, societies, and states; names of well-known persons who were members of the N.S.C.A.R.; and many of the major awards and honors received by members.

It is indeed unfortunate that I have been unable to locate or identify photographs of several of our early leaders, and understandably, some of the early records have been lost to time. I am, however, pleased to report that overall our records and history have been well preserved and are very complete. As we move into the next millennium we will leave behind a firm record of our past achievements for future generations to build upon.

As members of the N.S.C.A.R. we have a proud history to uphold. This book records the details of that history, and I am grateful to have had the opportunity to record this story of our past. I sincerely hope that readers will find *Centennial Plus One* to be of interest and use in future endeavors.

INTRODUCTION

On February 22, 1895, at the Fourth Continental Congress, of the National Society Daughters of the American Revolution, held in the Church of Our Father, Washington, District of Columbia, Mrs. Harriett Mulford Lothrop, the Regent of the Old Concord Chapter, Massachusetts, in a response to the address of the President General, N.S.D.A.R., Mrs. Stevenson, referred to the advisability of forming a young people's society, to be called Children of the American Revolution, *which would prepare children* to enter the ranks of the Daughters and Sons of the American Revolution. At that same Congress on the morning of the fourth day Mrs. Lothrop said:

> "The time remaining to us to complete the work of this Congress is so brief that the fewest words possible must be used to bring forward this great and important cause of the children and youth. The children and youth of America have a right to demand the opportunity to secure all these rights and privileges that help forward a perception and adoption of those American principles and institutions for which their ancestors fought and died. On whom does this responsibility rest, who will see to it that the children and youth have these rights and privileges which, by reason of their youth, they cannot claim and provide for themselves? Surely the women of America are, by their God-given offices of mother and sister, set apart to do this very work; and the Daughters of the American Revolution are again set apart from all other mothers and sisters because of their membership in this sacred cause for which this Society works. I appeal for the children and youth of America, and I add to my appeal this resolution:
>
>> 'Resolved, that the Society of the Children of the American Revolution shall be organized and adopted by the Daughters of the American Revolution.'"

The resolution was seconded by Mrs. Pryor, Miss Dorsey and Mrs. McLean, and others; and it was unanimously carried with great applause.

On Friday, April 5, 1895, at an adjourned meeting of the National Board of Management, DAR, with Mrs. John M. Foster, President General, presiding, Mrs. Lothrop addressed the Board and said it was "desirable that the Children's Society be under the control and direction of the 'Mother

Society,' the DAR, and requested the privilege of two small desks in the ante room for the use of the officers of the Children's Society."

The decision was reached that the term "Children of the American Revolution" could not be changed by the Board, and the Constitution of the Children of the American Revolution was adopted. It was decided by the founders that C.A.R. should be INCORPORATED in a SEPARATE ORGANIZATION and that its officers should be members in good standing in the DAR. Later this ruling was extended to include members in good standing in the Sons of the American Revolution and the Sons of the Revolution.

Harriett Mulford Lothrop
Concord, Massachusetts

Founder and First President
1895 – 1901

The National Society of the Children of the American Revolution was formally organized on April 5, 1895. The first Constitution and Bylaws were written.

CONSTITUTION

We, the children and youth of America, in order to know more about our country from its formation, and thus to grow up into good citizens, with a love for, and an understanding of the principles and institutions of our ancestors, do unite under the guidance and government of the Daughters of the American Revolution, in the Society to be called the NATIONAL SOCIETY OF THE CHILDREN OF THE AMERICAN REVOLUTION; and we adopt this Constitution.

ARTICLE I.

Any boy or girl may be eligible for membership in this Society from birth to the age of eighteen years for the girls and twenty-one years for the boys, who is descended from a man or woman who, with unfailing loyalty, rendered material aid to the cause of Independence; from a recognized patriot, a soldier or sailor or civil officer, in one of the several colonies or States, or of the United Colonies or States.

ARTICLE II.

We take as objects of this Society to work for: First, the acquisition of knowledge of American history, so that we may understand and love our country better, and then any patriotic work that will help us to that end, keeping a constant endeavor to influence all other children and youth to the same purpose. To help to save the places made sacred by the American men and women who forwarded American Independence; to find out and to honor the lives of children and youth of the Colonies and of the American Revolution; to promote the celebration of all patriotic anniversaries; to place a copy of the Declaration of Independence and other patriotic documents in every place appropriate for them; to hold our American Flag sacred above every other flag on earth. In short, to follow the injunctions of Washington, who in his youth served his country, till we can perform the duties of good citizens.

And to love, uphold and extend the institutions of American liberty and patriotism, and the principles that made and saved our country.

ARTICLE III.

The officers of this Society shall be a President and other officers. These shall be appointed, during her term, by the President who has been appointed by, and to whom has been given the organization and the care of this Society by the Daughters of the American Revolution. This first President to serve not less than four years.

The President and the other officers of the second term to be elected annually by ballot at the Continental Congress of the Daughters of the American Revolution, by a vote of the majority of the members of that body.

The meetings of the Board of Officers of the National Society of the Children of the American Revolution will be held in Washington, D.C., and may be one or two in a year, as agreed by the Board, the President having the right to call a special meeting if occasion demands.

ARTICLE IV.

All members of this Society shall pay an annual fee of fifty cents.

The fees of members at large shall go entire into the Treasury of the National Board of the Children of the American Revolution. The fees of young people forming local Societies are to be divided in the following manner:

Twenty-five cents to go to the National Fund of the Society, twenty-five cents to the local Societies.

The fee due the National Society must be sent to the Treasurer at the same time that the application for membership is forwarded to the Registrars.

Annual dues are to be paid in advance on or before the 22d of February of each year.

A separate National and Local Fund may be formed for the express purpose of preserving patriotic places and articles, as occasion permits and as voted by the Society.

ARTICLE V.

Local Societies assisted by the Daughters of the American Revolution, may be formed in any locality. The President of such

Society to be a Daughter of the American Revolution; the other officers to be young people who are members of the Society.

ARTICLE VI.

Any amendment to this Constitution may be offered at any meeting of the National Board of Management of the C.A.R., but shall not be acted upon until the next meeting thereof, when it shall be settled by a majority vote of the members present.

BY-LAWS.

I.
REGULAR MEETINGS.

The regular meeting of the National Board of Management shall be held at the Board Room, on the first Tuesday of each month, with the exception of July, August and September, at ten o'clock. Five members shall constitute a quorum.

II.
ANNUAL MEETING.

The annual meeting shall be in Washington, D.C., on February 22d. All business not considered appropriate for the National holiday, to be transacted on another day of same week, as agreed upon by the Board of Management.

III.
NAMES OF LOCAL SOCIETIES.

A name of a Local Society, once chosen by such Society, cannot be adopted by another Local Society. As soon as the name is selected, it must be at once reported to the Corresponding Secretary. Local Societies must be named for persons, or events, or places associated with the early history of our country. No later date than 1820 can be allowed. As far as possible, the names of girls and boys who helped forward the cause of American Independence should be adopted.

IV.
The Seal.

The seal of the Society has upon its face the figures of a girl and boy in dress appropriate to the Continental period. Between them is the shield. Above them are thirteen stars arranged in a symbolic setting. Around the rim is the legend, Children of the American Revolution.

V.
Insignia.

The insignia of the Society is a solid silver pin overlaid with gold, the outer rim is a garter of heraldic blue enamel carrying the legend Children of the American Revolution, ending with a buckle. With wings outspread in the attitude of "Old Glory," the eagle occupies the center of the open space together with the flag, which he holds in his talons. The flag, in red, white and blue enamel, is draped, one-half with the stars on the blue field over the garter, and the end of red and white stripes floating back of the legend. The name and national number of each owner to be engraved on back of badge. The colors of the National Society of the Children of the American Revolution, shall be red, white and blue; the only other badge of the Society being a knot or ribbon or narrow red, white and blue ribbon.

VI.
Certificates

The certificate of the Society, on Japanese paper with border in sepia, commemorates with historic accuracy some of the principal events in our Nation's history, interweaving our motto, "For God and Country." The seal of the Society stamped on a red leather wafer is attached.

VII.
Charters

The charter for a local Society illustrates in sepia on Japanese paper the historic account of a meeting between Washington and a company of children, and the words he used on the occasion. The charter of a local Society may contain as many names of its organizing members as its space will allow.

VIII.
STATE PROMOTERS

There may be in each State such number of its best representative men and women as shall be considered advisable by the National Board of Management, who shall be ready to use all their influence toward the growth and prosperity of the Society, and thus be State Promoters of the Children of the American Revolution. These to be appointed by the National Board of Management and to serve during its pleasure.

REGULATIONS OF LOCAL SOCIETIES
Belonging to the
NATIONAL SOCIETY
of the
CHILDREN OF THE AMERICAN REVOLUTION

The President of each Society must belong to the National Society of the Daughters of the American Revolution. The other officers of each Society to be its young members. Children and youth of both sexes may become members.

A Director in each State, appointed by the National President, shall serve in that State. She must belong to the National Society of the Daughters of the American Revolution.

There can be as many societies in a city or town as may be authorized by the National Board. If possible, name Societies after girls or boys who did patriotic service in connection with the Revolutionary War, or period not later than 1820. It is one of the aims of this Society to find them. Any number of members may form a local Society as approved by its president.

There are two classes of members; those in Local Societies, who are known as Local Members, and those not joining through a Local Society, who are known as members at large.

Fees for all members per year, fifty cents.

Fees of Local Members to be thus divided: Twenty-five cents to go to Treasurer of National Society; twenty-five cents to go to Local Society. Fees of Members at Large go entire to Treasurer of National Society.

Fees must be sent by Treasurers of Local Societies on the 1st and 15th of each month, sending as many as possible at a time.

When requesting Application Blanks from the Corresponding Secretary, the applicant must enclose one cent in postage stamps, for each blank, to cover expenses of same.

When forwarding Application Blanks that have been filled out, to the Registrars, one two-cent stamp for the return of each duplicate blank must be enclosed.

Application papers, when filled out, must be forwarded by the Registrars of Local Societies to the Registrars of National Society on the 1st and 15th of each month. On these dates as many as possible should be sent.

For Application Blanks, Constitutions, Circulars and Printed matter, apply to Corresponding Secretary Mrs. Mary Sawyer Foote, 920 Massachusetts Avenue, N.W., Washington, D.C.

For Certificates and Badges apply to Registrar Mrs. Rosa Wright Smith, 1203 N st., NW., Washington, D.C. Badges $1.00, which includes engraved name, National number and registered postage. Certificates $1.00, which includes postage.

For Charters of Local Societies, apply to Recording Secretary, Mrs. Marcus Benjamin, Smithsonian Institution, Washington, D.C. Charters $3.00, which includes postage.

For permits for purchase of Stationery, apply to Vice-President in charge of Organization of Local Societies, Mrs. T. H. Alexander, 1207 N st., N.W., Washington, D.C.

When officers or members of Local Societies are writing to officers of the National Society, care must be taken to address the proper officer. Letters will be answered much more promptly and all confusion be avoided by carefully observing this regulation.

This concludes the original Bylaws.

☆ At an informal meeting, the firm of Bailey, Banks & Biddle of Philadelphia was asked to estimate the cost of badges; the Harrisburg Publishing Company was asked to supply application blanks and Certificates of Membership for the President's approval. A committee was formed to invite representatives in each state to serve as State Promoters.

☆ The *Boston Evening Transcript* published C.A.R. Leaflet, No. 1.

☆ Margaret Mulford Lothrop, daughter of our Founder, was made Member #1 on Flag Day, June 14.

Mrs. Lothrop, seated front center, with her N.S.C.A.R. Board members taken in 1895

Cover of C.A.R. Leaflet, No. 1 by the Boston Evening Transcript June 8, 1895

On July Fourth, 1895, the National Society of the Children of the American Revolution met in the Old South Meeting House, Boston, Massachusetts.

☆ *The Delineator Magazine* printed an article entitled "The Patriotic Societies.—No. 5. The National Society of the Children of the American Revolution," by Carolyn Halsted, in its September issue.

☆ On October 28th at a meeting held in Room 50 at 902 F Street, Washington, D.C., the Badge Committee Chairman reported that she had received designs of badges from several manufacturers. The J. E. Caldwell & Co. and Bailey, Banks & Biddle will meet with the Board.

☆ It was decided in November to have Bailey, Banks & Biddle manufacture certificates and badges and in December the wording for the certificate was accepted. In January, 1896, a motion was made and carried "that Local Societies be allowed to have charters."

☆ The official motto of the National Society, "For God and My Country," was adopted. The insignia and seal were approved.

☆ At the close of the first year's work, the membership was 318 with 58 societies, and four volumes of membership applications were bound. Bailey, Banks & Biddle presented the Board a badge with metal design which was approved as well as the stationery.

☆ February 22, 1896—Mrs. Lothrop rang a Petticoat Bell (which is in the C.A.R. National Museum) to open the First Congress. It was held in the

Margaret Mulford Lothrop at age eight years

Church of Our Father in Washington, D.C. The first lady of the nation, Mrs. Grover Cleveland received the C.A.R. members at the White House.
☆ It was decided to have the ribbon of the Society in the colors of red, white, and blue. The insignia was to be attached and suspended from a bar.
☆ Room 48 of the Loan and Trust Building in Washington, D.C., was rented for $25.00 monthly starting April 15th. Bylaws were adopted.
☆ Following is the story of the C.A.R. Tree as told by Mrs. Lothrop:

> On the completion of the work of founding the National Society Children of the American Revolution, it seemed to me that the most important work to be done was to connect the living personality of Washington to the minds and hearts of the children, that they could not fail to recognize him as their friend of today.
>
> It was necessary therefore to lift him out of the pages of history into the realm of the living present, where they could see him, and honor and love him. How could it be done? Clearly only in one way. By making Mt. Vernon, his home, the place where the children could meet Washington the Father of his Country with the same simple delight as if they were actually going to Grandfather's old home where the family drew together in affectionate remembrance.
>
> The next question was, how could this be accomplished? Then the voice of the tree began to be heard, and it spoke to me! 'Nothing is so vital, so strong, so enduring as a tree! Oh, if only one can be planted

10

Official Insignia and Seal of the National Society of the Children of the American Revolution

there in the name of the children, what a marvelous appeal to the young people of our country it would be! They could not avoid its call. And going to his home, they could never forget that Washington was their loving, personal friend of today!'

But the vision of the C. A. R. Tree at Mt. Vernon seemed perilously near to fading, when I realized how difficult it was at that time to get the permission for the planting of trees there. But, then I also realized that nothing was hopeless that concerned the Children's cause. It never is, and it never will be, and so I put the case before the Regents of Mt. Vernon.

They responded with prompt courtesy, not only granting the permission, but more. They asked where I would like the tree to be planted. I replied on the greensward midway between the mansion and the old Tomb where Washington was in the habit of pacing to and fro to gaze across the Potomac.

It seemed to me most fitting that a tree, taken from near the old North Bridge at Concord, Massachusetts, where Emerson said, 'Was fired the shot heard round the world,' should express this tribute, and one of the leading patriotic citizens of the old Colonial town, Mr. Charles W. Prescott, gladly recognizing this, effected the work of taking up the tree and its transportation to Mt. Vernon.

In 1896, the Annual Convention was held, as was that of the Daughters of the American Revolution, in February during the week in which Washington's birthday occurred. As no planting was permissible in that season, the sacred soil taken from around the tree, was sent on, and with appropriate ceremonies witnessed by a large circle of patriotic citizens, and the group of the newly fledged C.A.R. Society, the ground was broken, and the sacred soil laid within.

To Colonel Harrison H. Dodge, the Superintendent of Mt. Vernon, we were indebted, and shall ever be, for the presence here of this living tribute to Washington. From that 22nd of February, 1896, he has been the constant protector of this Tree, the emblem of the love and veneration of the C.A.R. for Washington.

On April 19, 1896, he planted the tree in this spot, and telegraphed me the joyful fact. We were holding a mass meeting in the old Parish 'Continental Church' at Concord, Massachusetts, waiting for the news. Up-borne by the booming of the cannon and the ringing of the bells that always proclaimed the end of the celebration of that historic birthday, the dawn of the American Republic, was flashed over the wires by Colonel Dodge. 'The Children American Revolution Tree was planted at high noon today at Washington's Home, Mt. Vernon!'

The tree had many vicissitudes and some experiences that sorely threatened its young life. Blizzards and other storms attacked it. Colonel Dodge watched and cared for it with unremitting fidelity and brought it through to vigor and beauty. To him we owe the life of this Tree, the C.A.R. tribute to Washington.

☆ During May of 1896, a patent was received for the C.A.R. insignia and ribbon. There were gifts to the society of eight chairs as well as the framing of the Constitution.

☆ In October the next volume of 800 applications was bound. Mrs. Lothrop proposed that the National Society of the Children of the American Revolution should have a publication in the nature of a Bulletin.

☆ In 1897, the Second Annual Convention was held during the week of George Washington's birthday at the Columbian University Hall, corner of 15th & H Streets, Washington, D.C.

☆ Throughout the year many events took place. Arrangements were made for the Children of the American Revolution to be present at the Nashville Exposition. The First Convention Of All Patriotic Societies In New England took place in North Conway, New Hampshire, and Mrs. Lothrop spoke on "Children of the American Revolution."

☆ The Tennessee Daughters of the American Revolution invited the N.S.C.A.R. to participate in the Tennessee Centennial. They met to commemorate Yorktown Day with great pomp and ceremony at Nashville, Tennessee. Seven Tennessee C.A.R. Societies took part and Mrs. Lothrop spoke. Members of the C.A.R. presented a "Flag of Liberty" Tableau. Miss Margaret Lothrop responded to this tribute.

☆ These are the words to *Our Flag of Liberty* written by Mrs. Lothrop and were used in the opening exercises of the societies:

> Our country's flag, to thee we give
> Our heart's devotion while we live;
> Symbol of all that makes us free,
> To thee we render loyalty.
>
> In every crimson waving stripe
> We see devotion's prototype;
> With all our heart's blood we'll defend
> Our dear old flag unto the end.
>
> And white as yonder fluttering bar
> We'll keep our souls in peace or war,
> That we may ever worthy be,
> O flag, to live or die for thee.
>
> True as the field of blue we'll be,
> And serve our country faithfully.
> Devotion, purity and truth
> Shall form the vanguard of our youth.
>
> Then stars like thine, with radiant light,
> Shall make this land of promise bright,
> When all her youth shall loyal be
> To thee, O flag of liberty.

☆ A motion passed to allow Honorary Membership provided said person was a member of either D.A.R., D.R.[1], S.A.R., or S.R. The Board passed a motion to allow parents to retire their children from membership whenever they so desire.

☆ Three hundred copies of the revised constitution were ordered and 400 postal cards with insignia of the Society for the President and her officers to use.

☆ Following is "The Story of Your Charter" by Harriett M. Lothrop:

> I have many times related to patriotic assemblies the history illustrated by the beautiful sketch on the Charters issued by our National Society of the Children of the American Revolution. Our National Board C.A.R. has now requested me to write it for publication in leaflet form, a copy of which is to be sent to each Society as a further inspi-

---

[1]Daughters of the Revolution of 1776 was organized in 1891 but has since been dissolved.

ration toward the best development of our children and youth as desired by the Father of our Country.

Very soon after I founded the National Society C.A.R., I chose its motto and then I began to search for a true, historic basis for a sketch for the Charter. I consulted every possible authority on Washington and his time. At last, at the Congressional Library, I found the following, which I copied from the volume, giving the story with suggestions for the sketch to be prepared. This when completed I laid before our National Board C.A.R., and it was accepted.

From *Memoirs of His Own Time, Including the Revolution, the Empire, and the Restoration* by Lieut.-Gen. Count Mathieu Dumas, in two volumes, London: 1839, Vol 1, pp.32-33.[2]

"General Washington and General Rochambeau decided on passing the whole of the winter (1780-81) in passive observation, always holding themselves ready to profit by the most favourable circumstances which might present themselves. The whole of this comparative suspension of hostilities was well employed in putting the American Army in good condition for the opening of the campaign; and General Rochambeau, on his side, who was expecting the arrival of a second division, prepared himself to aid our allies with vigor. General Washington, accompanied by the Marquis de la Fayette, repaired in person to the French headquarters. We had been impatient to see the hero of Liberty. His dignified address, his simplicity of manner, and mild gravity, surpassed our expectation, and won every heart. After having conferred with Count Rochambeau, as he was leaving us to return to his headquarters near West Point, I received the welcome order to accompany him as far as Providence. We arrived there at night; the whole of the population had assembled from the suburbs; we were surrounded by a crowd of children carrying torches, reiterating the acclamations of the citizens; all were eager to approach the person of him whom they called father, and pressed so closely around us that they hindered us from proceeding. General Washington was much affected, stopped a few moments, and pressing my hand said: 'We may be beaten by the English; it is the chance of war; but behold an army which they can never conquer.'"

From diligent search among authorities, I have never been able to find any earlier mention of Washington as "Father," the honor doubtless belonging to this little band of children grouped to reverently welcome him in 1780.

[2]Count Dumas was an aide-de-camp to General Rochambeau.

Painting of George Washington and children on our charter

The Children of the American Revolution is indeed an Army that can never be conquered.

☆ The Treasurer was requested to furnish the Board with a list of names and amounts of money contributed by the Children of the American Revolution for the Continental Hall Fund.

☆ A motion was passed that the new Article IV of the Constitution be omitted until the further revision of the Constitution.

☆ The Third Annual Convention was held at the Columbian University during the week of February 17-23, 1898. Ohio and Pennsylvania had a project to raise money for the Spanish-American War relief fund. A note of thanks was given to Mrs. McCleeman for her book "A Daughter of Two Nations." The exercises in honor of Washington's birthday were held at the Columbia Theatre.

☆ Gavel ceremonies included the History of the Handle, History of the Hammer and Presentation of the Gavel to the National Society by Margaret Mulford Lothrop of Concord, Massachusetts, and Sarah Smith Howard of Alexandria, Virginia, and accepted by the National President,

Following is the history of the gavel:

> The finished gavel arrived in Washington the very day of its delivery to the Society. But during the months of waiting, the plan for the gavel grew. Why not have the wood from the homes of the first four Virginia Presidents?
>
> Mrs. Eleanor Washington Howard had been present, the last daughter born at Mt. Vernon and being asked, she went to Mt. Vernon and got a piece of magnolia, the last tree Washington's hand had planted and which had been blown down in a storm the winter before.
>
> The obtaining of the Jefferson piece was easy. Miss Caroline Randolph of "Edgehill" and her brother, Dr. Wilson Cary Nicholas Randolph, great, grandchildren of Jefferson, united in giving a fragment from the table upon which Jefferson's telescope had rested as he watched the building of the University of Virginia, his "darling child."
>
> Through Miss Lelia Madison Baker, great-niece of President Madison, Dr. James Madison, his great-nephew, still living then at Montpelier, sent part of a tree from the old avenue.
>
> It took some time and effort to find the nearest of kin to President Monroe; but finally, with a very gracious letter from Mrs. Ruth Monroe Gouverneur Johnson, came a delightfully interesting bit of the walnut desk Mr. Monroe used when Minister to France during the French Revolution and brought back from Paris.

The Miller Manual Labor School, in Albemarle County, had an expert carver to instruct the boys; and he kindly undertook to carve and put together these historic souvenirs, making the Hammer carving thus:

Washington	Mt. Vernon
Jefferson	Monticello
Madison	Montpelier
Monroe	Monroe Hill

the finishing band to go between.

The expense of the final setting by Messrs. Bailey, Banks & Biddle of Philadelphia, was generously borne by the Albemarle Chapter, D.A.R. of Charlottesville, Virginia, of which Mrs. Sampson was a member; at a cost of $20.00, if memory serves.

The great jewelers with zealous enthusiasm made the gavel gorgeous with silver gilt, with the Arms of the United States emblazoned in colorful enamel; and engraved upon it the names of the contributors.

The occasion of the presentation was brilliant. The great audience in the old Columbia Theatre, lights and flowers and gay, happy faces. Two addresses were made. One for Massachusetts by Mr. Wm. B. Bradford. a descendant of Governor Bradford. The other for Virginia by Professor John Russell Sampson.

The beautiful and historic emblem of authority was carried upon the stage and delivered to the President of the National Society by two little girls, Margaret Mulford Lothrop, daughter of the National President C.A.R. and the very first member of the very first society, the North Bridge, and Sarah Smith Howard, daughter of Mrs. Eleanor Washington Howard, of Mt. Vernon birth.

☆ On February 25, the President and Mrs. William McKinley received the National Officers and members of the Society at the Executive Mansion.

☆ Also during, February it was decided that no proxy be allowed at the National Board meetings. Another motion passed that a committee be appointed to nominate officers for the ensuing term, such committee to be appointed by the President after the delegates had arrived.

☆ The Fourth Annual Convention held February 17-23, 1899, at Columbian University Hall, Washington, D.C., included the Observance of Washington's Birthday at the Columbia Theatre on the 22nd.

Gavel made from pieces of wood representing the homes of the first four Virginia Presidents

☆ It was moved, seconded and carried that medals would be sent to the young members of the National Society C.A.R. who took part in the Spanish-American War.

☆ The State Director of New York presented an hereditary badge of membership in the "Mary Washington Monumental Association" to the National President.

☆ President and Mrs. William McKinley again received the National Board of Management C.A.R. and its visiting members at the Executive Mansion.

☆ The following is in reference to National Projects:

The local Societies which belong to the National Society of the Children of the American Revolution often desire specific work aside from that connected with their town or State history. They may unite their interests with other patriotic Societies engaged in forwarding the National Movements toward erecting Memorials in honor of Revolutionary heroes.

For the year 1899-1900, there has therefore been added to the Continental Memorial Hall Work, to which the Children of the American Revolution have generously contributed in the past, and will so continue to do, the work connected with the erection of the

Lafayette Statue, and also the Washington Statue, both to be unveiled at Paris during the Exposition in 1900; also the work connected with the Monument to be raised to the Memory of the Prison Ship Martyrs at Fort Greene, New York.

These two pieces of work are laid out in response to the many requests of the young Members of the National Society all over the Country; their adoption of course to be optional. They are in nowise to be considered obligatory, but as suggestions rather to those who desire definite plans of work other than the usual routine society work. To be valuable at all, the effort must be a voluntary one. Only in this way can the work become the inspiration which it is believed and hoped will result in many contributions to these objects.

All communications concerning the Lafayette Statue Fund, or the Washington Statue Fund, and all money for either object, should be forwarded to Mrs. William Cummings Story, Hatfield Hall, Lawrence, Long Island, New York, Chairman of the Franco-American Committee of the N.S.C.A.R.

All communications concerning the Fund for the Monument to the Prison Ship Martyrs and all money for this object, should be forwarded to Mrs. Charles E. Sprague, 116 West 75th St, N.Y., Chairman of the Prison Ship Martyrs Memorial Committee of the N.S.C.A.R.

Entertainments of varied descriptions should be planned by local societies if they intend to take up any of the above work. The Summer months should be utilized for lawn fetes and garden parties, and other recreations appropriate to the vacation season.

☆ The Fifth Annual Convention again took place at the Columbian University on February 17, 1900.

☆ It was decided that "Hereafter State Directors shall be allowed the privilege of voting at the National Board meetings."

☆ Presentation of the medals to members who volunteered for the Spanish-American War took place. The "Halls of the Ancients" were opened to the Society for a fee and young members of the District of Columbia Societies appeared in fancy costumes. One-half of the receipts were donated to the Continental Hall fund of the Daughters of the American Revolution.

☆ President William McKinley received the National Board of Management, Children of the American Revolution, and its visiting members at the Executive Mansion.

☆ Mrs. Lothrop, National President, was designated by the National Board of Management to represent the National Society at the Paris Exposition of 1900.

☆ The Sixth Annual Convention, held in 1901, was the last one at which Mrs. Lothrop presided. The society had grown to 33 states and territories with 162 Societies.

☆ The Constitution and By-laws were amended again.

☆ The President and Mrs. William McKinley, with the ladies of the Cabinet, received the National Board of Management with the visiting members at the Executive Mansion.

☆ Mrs. Tunis Hamlin, Chaplain, requested the privilege of making a statement, and motion as follows:

> Resolved, That in view of the fact that Mrs. Daniel Lothrop is now retiring from the Presidency of the National Society of the Children of the American Revolution, her eminent services for the Society in giving so generously of her time, ability and means in founding the Organization and in bringing it to its present state of success, be recognized by appropriating such an amount of money from the National Treasury as the National Board shall decide, to buy and present to her, as a testimonial, such a medal. as they may select, to be kept by her as a memorial and be given to her descendants, as a testimonial of our appreciation and regard for her eminent and valuable services to the Society during the six years of its organization—Seconded and agreed to by the Convention.

> It was moved that, in view of the long, untiring and priceless services of Mrs. Daniel Lothrop in founding and organizing this Society, it is hereby ordered that during her entire life she shall be a Honorary President, or President Emeritus of the Society with the rights of full membership in the National Board, and in every convention which she may hereafter attend. Seconded and unanimously carried by the Convention.

☆ The new National President, Mrs. George M. Sternberg, was elected.

1901–1903

National President
Mrs. George M. Sternberg
Wisconsin

☆ During her term of office, Mrs. Sternberg appointed a Chairman of Editing Committee for the Monthly Bulletin, Children of the American Revolution. The Constitution was revised. The Board accepted the design for a badge to be presented to Mrs. Daniel M. Lothrop, Honorary President, submitted by Bailey, Banks & Biddle. The badge to cost $100.00. In June 1901, the jeweled badge was presented to Mrs. Lothrop.

☆ Interesting matters of our society were sent to the American Monthly Magazine which were published. The society ordered 50 yearly subscriptions to the magazine. The heading of the Young People's Department in the magazine was changed to the National Society Children of the American Revolution.

☆ The Connecticut C.A.R. raised $250.00 of the $500.00 required for a monument at Groton Heights erected by the Daughters of the American Revolution.

☆ The Seventh Annual Convention was also held at the Columbian University in 1902. At this time, the membership included 5,400 enrolled members. The National Board was received at the White House by President and Mrs. Theodore Roosevelt.

☆ The Society of the Sons of the American Revolution in the District of Columbia amended its constitution so that the members of the Society of the Children of the American Revolution could now become members of the S.A.R. without initiation fee.

☆ A flag was presented to the Woman's League of the National Junior Republic near Annapolis, Maryland, by the National Society of the Children of the American Revolution.

☆ The National Registrar was authorized to employ clerical assistance during the summer months, or as long as such assistance be needed.

☆ In 1903, the Eighth Annual Convention was held during the week of George Washington's Birthday with the usual program. Membership is now up to 5,841. Margaret Lothrop, Member #1, reached the age limit (eighteen) and transferred to the Daughters of the American Revolution.

☆ The new National President, Mrs. Julius C. Burrows, was elected.

1903–1905

National President
Mrs. Julius C. Burrows
Grand Rapids, Michigan

☆ A "Colonial Tea" was given by the National Board of Management at the Washington Club, 1710 I Street, NW, in honor of the visiting members of the National Society of the Children of the American Revolution. A suggestion was made that the Children of the American Revolution be asked to contribute money for a memorial window in Continental Hall was acknowledged.

☆ The necessity of moving headquarters for the Board of Management was discussed. It was moved and carried that the Corresponding Secretary write the American Security and Trust Company in regard to securing a place of safety for the storage of papers, etc. No room in the building was available. She was requested to consult with the National Officers of the Daughters of the American Revolution and ascertain if the Board would be allowed to meet in a room at the Loan and Trust Building. It was decided to use half of a room for nine dollars a month at the present time.

☆ The bylaws were amended to change the date of National Convention from February 22 to April 19. The National Convention of the National Society of the Children of the American Revolution could then be held at the time of the National Congress of the Daughters of the American Revolution.

☆ It was moved and carried that the cut of a gold card presented to President William McKinley by a society in California be reproduced for the Smithsonian Report. The report of the Society is in Part 3 in the annual report of the Daughters of the American Revolution to the Secretary of the Smithsonian Institution.

☆ The President General of the Daughters of the American Revolution set aside 150 seats for the Children of the American Revolution at the ceremonies attendant upon the laying of the cornerstone of Continental Memorial Hall on April 19th.

☆ President and Mrs. Theodore Roosevelt received the Society in the East Room of the White House.

CEREMONIES
OF THE LAYING OF THE
CORNER STONE

APRIL·19·1904

NATIONAL SOCIETY
1890 — DAUGHTERS OF THE · 1904
AMERICAN REVOLUTION

13TH CONGRESS

D A R

MEMORIAL
CONTINENTAL HALL
WASHINGTON
·D·C·

Program cover for the Ceremonies of the Laying of the corner stone

✮ The Ninth Annual Convention convened in the Church of the Covenant, Washington, D.C., on April 20, 1904. Mrs. Lothrop, Honorary President and Founder, made the address of welcome, saying in part:

"While we are gratified at the attendance this morning, we can very well appreciate the fact that more children would be with us were it not for the schools being in session. I congratulate you all that you are able to be present at the ninth annual convention of the Society. Your presence in Washington is greatly appreciated by the parent organization, the Daughters of the American Revolution. You may very well feel proud of the important part you played yesterday in the patriotic services incident to laying the cornerstone of the Continental Memorial Hall which is to be your future home, and which you in the "kindergarten" so to speak, are to take care of as you grow up and become members of the Daughters of the American Revolution, taking places of those who are called to the great beyond. . ."

✮ Mrs. Sternberg, Chairman of the Ways and Means Committee, National Society Daughters of the American Revolution, urged that the Children of the American Revolution be enlisted to sell copies of the pictures of Memorial Continental Hall for the benefit of the building fund.

✮ The Society moved to larger quarters in the Loan and Trust Building at the increased rent of $3.50 per month for the new room for official headquarters.

✮ National Project: St. Louis, Missouri—Trans-Mississippi Exposition N.S.C.A.R. Exhibit—C.A.R. Day September 11, 1904.

✮ The Little Men and Women of '76 Society of Brooklyn, New York, had
31
raised the largest amount of money for Memorial Continental Hall and was presented the Loving Cup by Mrs. John Miller Horton of Buffalo, New York.

✮ The Tenth Annual Convention was held April 16-19, 1905. The new National President, Mrs. Frederick T. Dubois, was elected.

1905–1909

National President

Mrs. Frederick T. Dubois
Blackfoot, Idaho

☆ The National Society Daughters of the American Revolution decided to admit all applicants who have been members of the Children of the American Revolution to the parent Society without fee.

☆ A motion carried that the President appoint a committee of three ladies to act with the Treasurer to investigate the matter of selecting a room in Continental Hall for the Children of the American Revolution with power to take whatever action necessary.

☆ The President reported that she had appeared before the National Board of Management, D.A.R., at its last meeting, and conferred with the ladies on the subject of the Children's Room in Continental Hall. She found them interested in the junior Society and was told that a desirable room in the building was already set apart for its use.

She also spoke of the postal cards of the Hall which are sold for its benefit and suggested that some be made of the Children's Room in order that the members of the Society may have something to show that it really exists.

☆ The Trenton-Princeton Society, C.A.R., New Jersey, presented a table to be used in the room for the Children in Continental Hall. John Hart Society, Pittsburgh, Pennsylvania, purchased a desk and chair also for the Children's Room. The Valentine Holt Society of San Francisco, California, received the Loving Cup from Mrs. George W. Baird for contributing the largest amount of money to the Children's Room. Contributions to the DAR Continental Hall Fund now total $2,219.13.

☆ The Eleventh Annual Convention was held April 16-19, 1906 at the Chapel of the Church of the Covenant, Connecticut Avenue and N Street, NW, Washington, D.C.

☆ C.A.R. National Headquarters are now in Room 406, Washington Loan and Trust Building, 9th and F Streets, NW., Washington, D.C.

☆ Colorado became the first State Society in 1907.

☆ The children arranged to celebrate the 300th Anniversary of the first permanent English settlement in America on May 13th.

☆ The DAR Continental Hall fund is now $2,556.93.

☆ Mrs. Lothrop was requested to draft and send to the Peace Congress, convened in New York, a resolution endorsing the movement.

☆ The Twelfth Annual Convention was held in the Sunday School room of the Congregational Church on April 21, 1907.

☆ The Annual Pilgrimage to Mt. Vernon by steamboat was a joy as always. This year all members under fifteen years of age were admitted free. A wreath was placed at the tomb of George Washington by Mrs. Dubois, National President.

☆ The property of the Society was packed and moved from Room 406, Washington Loan and Trust Building to the Juvenile Court Building, 1816 F Street, NW, Washington, D.C.

☆ A Press Committee was formed and a scrapbook purchased for the important letters and cards.

☆ The Secretary was authorized to request the editor of the *American Monthly Magazine* (the publication of the Daughters of the American Revolution) to print the list of National Officers of the C.A.R. in each issue of the magazine.

☆ The Thirteenth Annual Convention held in April 1908 was also at the Congregational Church.

After placing a wreath, members and friends attending the Annual Pilgrimage to Mt. Vernon in 1907 pose in front of the tomb of George Washington

☆ A $5.00 gold piece was presented to Miss Allen in recognition of her valuable assistance in arranging the minuet danced at the Society's reception during Convention week.

☆ Bailey, Banks & Biddle was requested to present designs for revolutionary ancestor bars for the children to wear.

☆ The President and Mrs. William Howard Taft received the children at the White House.

☆ Mrs. Eleanor Seldon Washington Howard presided at the October Board since the President and Vice President were absent.

☆ The accumulation of the Society's papers were sorted. Those which were worthless were destroyed; those which proved valuable were filed. Programs, newspapers articles, photographs, etc. which were of interest were placed in a history book.

☆ On January 14, 1909, the Schuyler Society of Albany, New York, presented to the National Society Children of the American Revolution, a booklet entitled: *Leading Events of the American Revolution.*

☆ In February, 1909, Stella Bartholomew, member of the Society from Occidental, California, received a Life Saving medal from the U. S. Treasury Department in recognition of her services in rescuing a young man from drowning.

☆ The Fourteenth Annual Convention was held in the Sunday School room of the First Congregational Church, Washington, D.C., on April 19, 1909. The new National President, Mrs. Albert Baird Cummins, was elected.

1909–1918

National President

Mrs. Albert Baird Cummins
Des Moines, Iowa

☆ The children were eligible to have bars for each ancestor for whose service they have filed papers. Bailey, Banks & Biddle presented designs for them.

☆ A letter from Gen. Anthony Wayne of Revolutionary fame was presented to the N.S.C.A.R. as a gift from the State Director of Pennsylvania.

☆ The State Director for the District of Columbia spoke of the desirability of having in the District D.A.R. a committee on the C.A.R. and stated that she would urge the formation of a local C.A.R. society with each D.A.R. Chapter.

☆ Mrs. Daniel Lothrop and her daughter, Miss Margaret Lothrop, as Chairman of the special committee in charge of furnishing the Children's Room, in DAR Continental Hall, were empowered to act freely and entirely according to their judgment in the selection, purchase and placing of the furniture and decorations. The Treasurer was authorized to pay all bills. Suitable furniture in all solid mahogany was purchased which included a library table, corner cupboard, bookcase, desk and four chairs.

☆ Several C.A.R. Societies were busy at this time, such as:

The James Noble Society, Colorado Springs, Colorado, contributed funds toward the monument to be erected in memory of Samuel Champlain; in recognition of which each member of the Society received a gold medal from the Commission for the Public Celebration of the Tercentenary of the Discovery of Lake Champlain.

Carolina Marshall Wheelock Society, Danbury, Connecticut, raised money for a bronze tablet for the gate of an iron fence the DAR erected around an ancient cemetery.

Signal Lantern Society, Newtonville, Massachusetts, contributed money to the "Paul Revere Association" for windows in the living-room of "Paul Revere House."

☆ When the DAR built Memorial Continental Hall in 1910, the N.S.C.A.R. was given the privilege of buying one room "for their permanent use and occupancy forever."

The following is an exact copy of a hand-written note in the folder marked "C.A.R. Board Room" in the Business Office, N.S.C.A.R.:

$1105.00   Washington, D.C.
                            April 1910

Received of Violet Blair Janin, Treasurer of the National Society of the Children of the American Revolution, eleven hundred and five dollars to complete the payment in full for the room of the Children of the American Revolution in Memorial Continental Hall, for their permanent use and occupancy forever.

Signed,
Julia G. Scott, Pres. Gen. NSDAR
Signed,
Lula Reed Hoover, Treas. Gen. NSDAR

☆ The Fifteenth Annual Convention was held in the Children's Room April 18-23, 1910. The remaining Annual Conventions under the Presidency of Mrs. Cummins were all held in the Children's Room.

☆ The manager of the *Daughters of the American Revolution Magazine* said that hereafter C.A.R. matters would be published in the magazine.

☆ It was proposed to start a fund to purchase a portrait of Mrs. Lothrop to be hung in the Children's Room.

☆ A large bunting flag to float over the boys' summer home of the Home of the Friendless located at Alpsville, Pennsylvania, was given by the John Hart Society in Pittsburgh.

☆ Life membership was discussed. Since membership is limited by the age of the member, there was not a life membership but that the amount of the dues covering that period of time could be paid at one time. Since then, Life Membership was instituted and is still in effect.

☆ In the early part of 1912, there was a discussion about printing a C.A.R. magazine, which would cost $120.00 a year for 500 copies if issued quarterly. A description of the contents was made and 20 subscriptions had already been received.

The new publication *Children of the American Revolution Magazine* became a reality on February 22, 1912. The subscription price was twenty-five cents per year. It has always been a quarterly magazine containing articles of interest and describing the patriotic work of the children.

☆ Bailey, Banks & Biddle Company was chosen as the Official Jeweler.

☆ Three silver loving cups will be awarded during the Annual Convention.

☆ A C.A.R. Hymn was presented by Governor Thomas Welles Society, District of Columbia, to be used with Mrs. Lothrop's poem, *Our Flag of Liberty*, as a part of the salute to the flag at all meetings.

☆ A plate from the Washington china was presented by Miss Heth.

☆ A wreath was placed at the tomb of George Washington at Mt. Vernon. There was a patriotic ceremony by the tree planted by the Capital Society, D.C.

☆ The National President, Mrs. Cummins, offered a medal to the child which brings in the greatest number of new members. Our Founder, Mrs. Lothrop, offered a silver pitcher to the member who brings in the largest number of new members.

☆ A large tent was given to the Tuberculosis Association of Washington, D.C., to be used in helping the children who come under their care. A musical was given for the blind by the members of the Capital Society, D.C., in the Public Library.

☆ A motion was passed that hereafter the names of local Societies must relate to the Revolutionary period or the early history of the locality in which the Society is founded.

☆ The Carolina Marshall Wheelock Society of Danbury, Connecticut, entertained sixteen children from the Home of Orphans.

☆ The society will continue to bind the magazines each year.

Cover of Vol. 1., No. 1 of the Children of the American Revolution Magazine dated February 22, 1912.

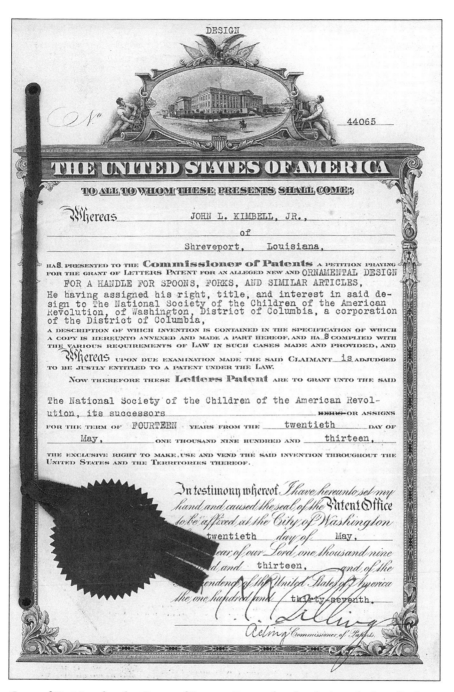

DESIGN

N°

44065

THE UNITED STATES OF AMERICA

TO ALL TO WHOM THESE PRESENTS SHALL COME:

Whereas JOHN L. KIMBELL, JR.,

of

Shreveport, Louisiana,

HAS PRESENTED TO THE **Commissioner of Patents** A PETITION PRAYING FOR THE GRANT OF LETTERS PATENT FOR AN ALLEGED NEW AND ORNAMENTAL DESIGN FOR A HANDLE FOR SPOONS, FORKS, AND SIMILAR ARTICLES,

He having assigned his right, title, and interest in said design to The National Society of the Children of the American Revolution, of Washington, District of Columbia, a corporation of the District of Columbia,

A DESCRIPTION OF WHICH INVENTION IS CONTAINED IN THE SPECIFICATION OF WHICH A COPY IS HEREUNTO ANNEXED AND MADE A PART HEREOF, AND HAS COMPLIED WITH THE VARIOUS REQUIREMENTS OF LAW IN SUCH CASES MADE AND PROVIDED, AND

Whereas UPON DUE EXAMINATION MADE THE SAID CLAIMANT is ADJUDGED TO BE JUSTLY ENTITLED TO A PATENT UNDER THE LAW.

Now THEREFORE THESE **Letters Patent** ARE TO GRANT UNTO THE SAID

The National Society of the Children of the American Revolution, its successors OR ASSIGNS

FOR THE TERM OF FOURTEEN YEARS FROM THE twentieth DAY OF May, ONE THOUSAND NINE HUNDRED AND thirteen,

THE EXCLUSIVE RIGHT TO MAKE, USE AND VEND THE SAID INVENTION THROUGHOUT THE UNITED STATES AND THE TERRITORIES THEREOF.

In testimony whereof, I have hereunto set my hand and caused the seal of the Patent Office to be affixed at the City of Washington twentieth day of May, year of our Lord, one thousand nine hundred and thirteen, and of the Independence of the United States of America the one hundred and thirty-seventh.

Acting Commissioner of Patents.

Copy of Petition for the Grant of Letters Patent for the design of a handle for spoons, forks and similar articles for the National Society of the Children of the American Revolution dated May 20, 1913

Design for the Official Spoons of the National Society of the Children of the American Revolution by John Lamar Kimbell, Jr., of Shreveport, Louisiana.

It was decided to sell the forks and spoons in the C.A.R. Room the first day of DAR Continental Congress and in the DAR Museum afterwards.

☆ The following is an informative letter in reference to the Red Cross:

DEAR CHILDREN OF THE AMERICAN REVOLUTION:

I have the greatest confidence in each one of you that when a splendid duty calls you will rise to meet it gladly.

In the goodness of God, our beloved Country is at peace. Our children go to school, enjoy their homes, and their little worlds are undisturbed. Look at the countries across the sea, where War in all its cruel forms is slaughtering, burning, and destroying, till rivers of blood and countless ruined homes are left in its wake.

Members of the C.A.R., can't you see in your imagination those other children across the sea, whose fathers and brothers have given their lives to protect them, and to defend their Countries? Can't you realize how these children are fleeing from these dreadful places, that are all that remain of their dear homes? Let us, Children of the American Revolution, stretch out helping hands to them, and *at once*.

The following Resolution that I offered has been adopted by the National Board of the C.A.R.:

I move that the National Society of the Children of the American Revolution be identified with the Red Cross Society; and therefore recommend that the Presidents of the Local Societies include it in their plan of Patriotic work for the year.

In consultation with Miss Mabel T. Boardman, Chairman of the Executive Board of the Red Cross Society, who warmly appreciates the allegiance of our National Society, C.A.R. to the Red

Cross work, she has given me a printed list of articles needed, which is as follows:

CLOTHING NEEDED BY BELGIAN AND OTHER REFUGEE
WOMEN AND CHILDREN:
WOOLEN BLOUSES
WARM SKIRTS
BOOTS AND SHOES
STOCKINGS
COTTON CHEMISES—untrimmed
KNITTED MUFFLERS or SCARFS to cover head and shoulders

But ABOVE EVERYTHING, shawls, knitted, woven, or made of warm woolen material, large enough to fold so that they cover the head, and the shoulders and body as well.

They do not wear sweaters. Only the young girls will wear coats. Some will wear petticoats. These would be very useful for the children; also simple warm dresses, and knitted hoods, with long ends to throw around neck, or with short capes to cover shoulders.

Presents of yarn and long knitting needles would be very welcome. All the refugees beg for wool, etc.

The need for blankets is going to be overpowering this winter in Belgium, and in all war-ridden countries.

(Extract from a letter received by the American Red Cross from Belgium.)

Miss Boardman also sends me a cheesecloth pad (like enclosed pattern) which she thinks the children might fold. Absorbent gauge pads 9 inches square, 8 thicknesses, made from pieces of gauze 1 yard wide, ½ yard long, folded according to sample which will be sent on request, are also needed. Pads should be done up in packages of 25 and tied. These dressings need not be sterilized.

The above supplies should be packed separately and the contents of each package clearly stated on the outside. Shipments should be made to the American Red Cross, care Bush Terminal Company, 39th Street and Second Avenue, Brooklyn, New York.

She also suggests that the members of the C.A.R. should get up little entertainments to raise money. Send money, designating it for Red Cross, to Mrs. Violet Blair Janin, Treasurer Nat. Soc. C.A.R., 12 Lafayette Square, Washington, D.C.

All these contributions will go to the Belgian and other poor children suffering from the war.

Let me know your progress.

With best wishes for your success in, and devotion to, this work, I am, my dear C.A.R. Red Cross Band,

Always affectionately yours,
(signed, Harriett M. Lothrop)

Wayside	Founder Nat. Soc. C.A.R.
Concord, Massachusetts,	National Chairman C.A.R.
October, 1914	

☆ Darby Printing Company was authorized to print the *Children of the American Revolution Magazine*.

☆ It was moved and carried to accept the offer of a silver cup to be presented next year to the child writing the best paper on some historic event during the Revolution.

☆ The Amos Morris Society, New Haven, Connecticut, has sent a $50.00 scholarship for Merryville College, Tennessee, for over fifteen years. Members of the Fort Steuben Society, Jeffersonville, Indiana, sent Easter cards to each resident of the Old Ladies' Home.

☆ Connecticut became a State Society.

☆ The unveiling of Mrs. Daniel Lothrop's portrait, painted by Edmund C. Tarbell, took place in the Children's Room in the DAR Continental Memorial Hall at four o'clock on Tuesday, April the Twentieth, 1915.

Mrs. Lothrop requested that her portrait be sent to the Corcoran Art Gallery for exhibition. A Chippendale chair and a pottery vase were presented to the room.

☆ A silk Flag of the United States of America will be given to the Society sending in the most subscriptions to the *Children of the American Revolution Magazine*.

☆ Miss Helen Stout was appointed to represent the Children of the American Revolution at a conference on the bill, "Desecration of the Flag."

☆ During the first World War, Margaret Lothrop served in France with the Women's Unit of the Red Cross. Miss Mabel T. Boardman, Chairman of the Executive Board of the Red Cross Society, wrote a letter thanking the Children of the American Revolution for the generous gifts to the American Red Cross to be utilized for Belgium as the children desired.

☆ The Constitution and Bylaws were amended again.

☆ A prize of $10.00 will be given to the member of C.A.R. who will write most clearly and interestingly the reason why he or she loves the C.A.R.

A view of the Children's Room on the third floor of Continental Memorial Hall with Mrs. Lothrop's portrait

37

☆ A second bookcase was purchased for the Children's room.

☆ The *Children of the American Revolution Magazine* was entered in the Washington Post Office as second class matter saving more than $1.00 in postage.

☆ In 1916, an historical play called "Frau Philipse's Krullers" about the lives of the old Philipse and Van Cortlandt families was written by two members of the Philipse Manor Society, Yonkers-On-the Hudson, New York, and produced in historic Manor Hall for Keskeskick Chapter, D.A.R.

☆ A credential card was printed for members of the Society to use in entering the hall.

☆ Two lots on 16th Street, in Washington, D.C., were offered to the C.A.R. for cultivation and five adjoining ones will be used for gardening.

☆ Massachusetts became a State Society.

☆ Plans for the children to be active with the Red Cross and Navy Leagues. They might help making bandages, filling comfort bags, pasting, and cutting puzzle pictures, knitting surgical sponges, etc.

☆ Mrs. Janin, N.S.C.A.R. Treasurer, presented to the Board a volume of *American Orders and Societies and Their Decorations*, a gift from Bailey, Banks & Biddle.

☆ Use of the Children's Room will be allowed for sewing meetings.

☆ Through 1917 much was accomplished by numerous societies.

James Bibb Society, Helena, Montana, gave a fruit shower to the Orphans' Home at Thanksgiving.

Governor Thomas Welles Society, D.C., erected two drinking fountains in two public playgrounds—Henry Park and Willow Tree Alley.

Col. Ann Hawkes Hay Society, D.C., placed a permanent cement sand-box in Stanton Park for the local children.

The Captain Greenberry Dorsey Society, Baltimore, Maryland, gave money toward equipping a gymnasium at St. Mary's Seminary, St. Mary's, Maryland.

Members of the Nathan Beman Society, Plattsburg, Pennsylvania, do Red Cross work, rolling gauze bandages, etc., at regular meetings.

Col. Williams Society, Gaffney, South Carolina, gave money toward founding a school at Tamassee.

☆ Harriett M. Lothrop served as Chairman of the Committee on Cooperation with the C.A.R.

☆ Peck O' Pennies Fund was started to be sent to the "Children of the Frontier" in France.

☆ A card party and dance were given at the Cairo Hotel, Washington, D.C., for the benefit of the Conservation Committee of the D.A.R.

☆ Mrs. George Thatcher Guernsey, President General of the Daughters of the American Revolution, was invited to become a Vice President of the National Society. Mrs. Guernsey accepted her election to the National Board.

☆ A bronze tablet was dedicated:

To Past and Present Members

OF THE

Children of the American Revolution

Who Have Enlisted In Our Country's Service

This Honor Roll Is Lovingly Dedicated

(32 names are listed)

☆ The question of the income tax was answered by the fact that the C.A.R. Society was exempt from taxation as it was a patriotic organization.

☆ Permission was given to place the *Children of the American Revolution Magazine* for sale in DAR Continental Hall.

☆ A set of twelve volumes of *The Pepper Stories* was presented to the Children of the American Revolution by the author, Margaret Sidney, (Mrs. Lothrop). Since Harriett Lothrop's father, Sidney Stone, was of the old school and disapproved of women writing for publication, she chose the pen name "Margaret Sidney," In 1877, she wrote *Polly Pepper's Chicken Pie* which was published in a Boston magazine for youngsters. The next year, she contributed *Phronsie Pepper's New Shoes*. She continued the adventure stories of wholesome boys and girls as a series and later they were published in book form as Five Little Peppers and How They Grew.

☆ New York became a State Society.

☆ Mrs. Cummins presided at the 1918 Annual Convention on Friday, the 22nd and passed away several days later. Her funeral was held on Wednesday, April 27. This was indeed a sad occasion. No National President was elected to succeed Mrs. Cummins.

☆ Mrs. E. S. W. Howard, National Vice President, presided following the death of Mrs. Cummins.

☆ Fifty-eight more names were added to the Honor Roll.

☆ During this period, several societies were helping with the war relief:

The John and Dolly Scott Society, Quincy, Illinois, sent knitted garments to our soldiers and sailors in the service.

Schuyler Society, Albany, New York, sent money to the Belgium War Relief.

Iroquois Society, Rochester, New York, had a special interest in its own Base Hospital, Unit 19, and contributed funds to provide and fully equip a bed.

☆ It was voted to have 3,000 questionnaires printed for use in the societies all over the country and that a record would be kept of the individual work of each child during the war.

☆ Suitable membership cards were printed.

☆ In October, 1818, the National Board meeting was held with Mrs. Horace M. Towner, a Vice President, presiding.

☆ National Recording Secretary, Mrs. Frank S. Ray, called the November meeting to order and asked for nominations for chairman. Miss Hilda Fletcher was nominated and elected. The December meeting was called to order by Mrs. Howard after which Mrs. Fletcher assumed the chair.

☆ At the January 1919 meeting with Mrs. Howard presiding, it was decided that a change in the time of our Annual Convention be changed to either the week preceding or the week subsequent to the D.A.R. Congress.

☆ Mrs. Guernsey, President General, D.A.R., volunteered to have the record of the war activities of the C.A.R. published for circulation with the record of the war work accomplished by the D.A.R.

☆ Mrs. Howard presided at the February, March and April Board meetings.

☆ There was a lack of interest shown by the young men in the society after their girl friends had left to join the Daughters since the age limit is different in the S.A.R. and D.A.R. A recommendation to admit members at the age of eighteen was sent to the S.A.R.

☆ The Twenty-fourth Annual Convention was held in 1919 in the Children's Room. The next National President, Mrs. Frank W. Mondell, was elected on April 22, 1919.

1919–1925

National President

Mrs. Frank W. Mondell
New Castle, Wyoming

☆ A World War I plaque, dedicated to C.A.R. members who served in the war, was unveiled by Mrs. Lothrop in the C.A.R. Board Room.

The National Society
Children of the American Revolution
dedicate this tribute to those
members who served in the Great War
for the freedom of humanity
1917-1919

☆ Money was raised for chicken farms in France. $800.00 was sent and two farms were named District of Columbia Children of the American Revolution Farm and Washington, D.C. Farm.

☆ The prize to the society sending the largest number of contributions to the magazine was a framed copy of the American's Creed autographed by William Tyler Page, the author.

☆ Ninety-eight more names were added to the Honor Roll.

☆ The National President appointed the following committees:

Patriotic Education
Tribute to those members of the C.A.R. who served "overseas"
and the inscription thereon
Prepare Leaflet of Information
Auditing
Printing
Finance
Memorial Trees
Membership

☆ On November 22, 1919 the Columbia Society, Portland, Oregon, gave a pageant—"The Evolution of the Flag" to raise money for its work and made a donation to the Armenian Relief.

☆ Mrs. Guernsey, President General, D.A.R., gave Mrs. Mondell time on the D.A.R. Congress program to talk about the interests of the C.A.R.

☆ There was discussion about a Memorial Tree to be planted on D.A.R. grounds, April 17, 1920, with an appropriate marker.

25TH ANNIVERSARY

☆ The 1920 Annual Convention was the 25th Anniversary and the National Society was invited by the American Forestry Association to plant a tree in front of Memorial Continental Hall as a memorial to our C.A.R. members and graduates who served in The Great War.

☆ The large book, *Roll of Honor*, the record of the C.A.R. service during World War I, beautifully bound in leather, with heavy brass corners and clasps, was on exhibition all day.

☆ Mrs. Daniel Lothrop pledged $100 for Tamassee Industrial School in South Carolina which made the N.S.C.A.R. a Founder of the school.

☆ The C.A.R. Society in Georgetown, D.C., erected a stone marker on M Street marking the headquarters of General George Washington. Permission was granted to replace the stone marker, now in bad condition, with a bronze one.

The C.A.R. Oak is to the right growing near the curb at the south entrance to the DAR driveway. Credit: Washingtoniana Division, D.C. Public Library

☆ The National Board passed that State Directors may appoint members of the D.A.R. Society to assist them. They will be designated District Councillors.

☆ The Revision of the Constitution and Bylaws was accepted.

☆ The National Mary Washington Memorial Association was granted permission to use the Children's Room for its annual meeting.

☆ Society activities:

The Nellie Custis Society, Buffalo, New York, presented a Victrola, costing $200, to the U. S. Army Hospital, and supported two fatherless children in France.

Elisha Hubbard Society, Berkeley, California, furnished subscriptions to the *Children of the American Revolution Magazine* for the Free Public Libraries, at Alameda, Berkeley and Oakland.

The Col. Nicholas Ruxton Moore Society, Baltimore, Maryland, adopted a ten year old French orphan boy.

☆ A copy of *The American's Creed* by William Tyler Page, was framed for the Children's Room. A plan was suggested to have copies of *The American's Creed* framed and placed in school rooms by the C.A.R. societies followed by a program.

☆ The Twenty-sixth Annual Convention was held in the Children's room.

✩ On the same day, Mrs. Warren G. Harding, wife of the President of the United States, received the members at a reception in the White House. The youngest one there was William Perry Doing, 6 weeks old, grandson of Mrs. Clayton E. Emig, National Organizing Secretary.

✩ Because of the rain at Mt. Vernon, installation services were held on the large front porch of the mansion.

✩ Attention was called to the readers of the *Children of the American Revolution Magazine* in regard to the advertisements in the December issue and suggestions were made to patronize them.

✩ The members of the Col. Nicholas Ruxton Moore Society, Baltimore, Maryland, wrote to all Congressmen and Senators from Maryland and asked for their cooperation in saving Fort McHenry as a National Park.

✩ The C.A.R. Societies in Massachusetts contributed $100 to endow the Massachusetts C.A.R. bed in the Children's Hospital and purchased a rolling chair to carry patients out to the sun parlor.

✩ The S.A.R. admitted young men to their society at the age of 18 instead of 21.

✩ In 1922 the Twenty-seventh Annual Convention was held in the auditorium of the Red Cross Building. The Red Cross treated the members, attending the Convention, to a wonderful panoramic display of pictures taken in connection with the work of the Red Cross all over the world.

✩ Georgia became a State Society.

✩ In June of 1922 an agreement was made in regard to space in the new DAR Administration Building for a 10 year period with a payment of one

Picture taken at Mt. Vernon following the tree exercises in 1922 shows Mrs. E. S. W. Howard, Vice President presiding, of our Society; Colonel Harrison Dodge, Superintendent of Mt. Vernon; and Mrs. Daniel Lothrop

dollar by each organization. N.S.C.A.R. paid $1,000 toward the cost of finishing the room on the second floor.

☆ Miss Helen Abraham was employed as the first staff member and worked in the Board Room.

☆ During the Christmas season many C.A.R. societies gave gifts to the various hospitals for children, veterans, etc., as well as poor needy families.

☆ The Twenty-eighth and Twenty-ninth Annual Conventions were held in Memorial Continental Hall.

☆ More than 2,000 new members were enrolled. C.A.R. now had more than 20,000 members. There were sixty new societies and five were reorganized.

☆ Nebraska became a State Society.

☆ In April, 1923, Mrs. Benjamin G. Miller organized the Crete Society in Crete, Nebraska. She wanted to indoctrinate the young people with some constructive ideals of service and citizenship. In this spirit, they planted what was destined to be the first Living Christmas Tree, and placed the whole project under C.A.R. sponsorship. The roots were firmly fixed in historic soil brought from the grounds of Memorial Continental Hall, the Lincoln Memorial, and the Nation's Capitol.

☆ In June, C.A.R. moved into new offices in the Administration Building.

☆ On October 11, 1923, Ethel Vance Moser wrote *The C.A.R. Creed* which was adopted as follows:

> I believe in the Children of the American Revolution as an organization for the training of boys and girls in true patriotism and love of country, in order that they shall be better fitted for American Citizenship.
>
> As a descendant of the Founders of my Country, I believe that my birthright brings a responsibility to carry on their work and that, as the boys and girls of 1776 took an active part in the War for Independence, so the boys and girls of today have a definite work to do for their country.
>
> As a child of the Children of the American Revolution, I believe it is my duty to use my influence to create a deeper love of Country, a loyal respect for its Constitution and reverence for its Flag among the children with whom I come in contact.

☆ Mrs. Calvin Coolidge, wife of the President, received the C.A.R. at the White House.

☆ Dies for stationery sold for $1.00 each. The winner of the contest for the largest number of new subscribers to the *Children of the American Revolution Magazine* received a silver spoon.

This is our fine new room - the Business Room - where all the click-click machines detail our constantly increasing National work in 1923

☆ The kindergarten at Ellis Island was the especial care of the C.A.R.

☆ Beginning with the September issue of the *Children of the American Revolution Magazine*, the magazine would be published every other month at the cost of fifty cents for six issues.

☆ In 1924, the Old Customhouse at Yorktown, Virginia, was purchased by the Comte de Grasse Chapter DAR and many C.A.R. Societies donated funds toward the purchase and the restoration of the House.

☆ Members of the Derick Amerman Society, Fairmont, Nebraska, planted two Black Hill Spruce as Memorial Trees near the entrance gate of the cemetery in the name of its Society and in memory of two sons of Revolutionary soldiers buried there.

☆ Mrs. Daniel Lothrop, Founder and First President of the C.A.R. from 1895 to 1901, spent her last years in California near her daughter, who taught at Stanford University. Although she died in August 1924, a continent away from her beloved New England home, she was buried on Authors' Ridge in Sleepy Hollow Cemetery, Concord, Massachusetts. In September Signal Lantern Society of Brookline, Massachusetts, held joint memorial services for Mrs. Lothrop and Calvin Coolidge, Jr.

☆ The Thirtieth Annual Convention was held in 1925 in the Auditorium of the Red Cross Building across the street from the DAR Building. The next four conventions were also held there. A memorial service for Mrs. Lothrop was held. During the convention, photos of Mrs. Daniel Lothrop were sold for $1.25 for the "Building Fund."

☆ The National President presented a silk Flag of the United States of America to the society securing the largest number of new members from January 1 to March 31.

☆ Mrs. Calvin Coolidge, wife of the President, received the members at the White House.

☆ The new National President, Mrs. Josiah A. Van Orsdel, was elected.

1925–1929

National President

Mrs. Josiah A. Van Orsdel
Beatrice, Nebraska

☆ Gifts were sent to the Ellis Island school for the children of immigrants.

☆ There was a Junior Department for Little Patriots in the *Children of the American Revolution Magazine*.

☆ The children of Conrad Weiser Society, Reading, Pennsylvania, honored the man whose name they use by planting a red oak tree on the farm of the great Weiser. This old Pennsylvania homestead will become a park.

☆ A bronze tablet, placed on the south side of the doors to the Armory at Mercer Street and Bergen Avenue, Jersey City, New Jersey, was unveiled:

> This marks the site of the Home of Jane Tuers, a heroine of the American Revolution. Presented by Jane Tuers Society, C.A.R. 1925

☆ The members of the convention went by boat to Mt. Vernon, placed wreaths on the tomb of George and Martha Washington, and held installation exercises by the tree planted by the C.A.R

☆ Indiana became a State Society.

☆ Three societies reported erecting bronze tablets:

The Columbia Society of Portland, Oregon, placed a tablet in the court yard of the Portland Hotel and unveiled it on June 17, the tenth anniversary of the organization of the society. It read:

This Is The Site Of
THE FIRST PUBLIC SCHOOL
BUILDING
Erected by Taxation in Portland
1858
Marked by
COLUMBIA SOCIETY
Children of the American Revolution
1926

The Martin's Fort Society, Paris, Kentucky, completed a granite shaft with a bronze tablet inscribed:

At This Spring
Pioneers Camped in the
Year 1776, and so
Determined the Townsite
of Hopewell, Later Paris
Marked by the
Martin's Fort Society
Children of the American
Revolution
1926

Captain James Jack Society, Charlotte, North Carolina, erected a tablet bearing the following inscription:

This tablet marks the site of the
home of
Captain James Jack,
Revolutionary Patriot
Bearer of
The Mecklenburg Declaration of
Independence

To The
Continental Congress in Philadelphia
1775
Erected by
Captain James Jack Society
Children of the American Revolution
1926

☆ Officers' titles, Chairman of Books and Curator of Historical Objects changed in 1926 to National Librarian-Curator.

☆ The *C.A.R. Song* was written for a local society meeting in 1926 by Mrs. Charles (Martha Parkinson) Mills who was Senior President of the Diane Evans Society of Rensselaer, Indiana. A visitor from Illinois and her daughter liked the song so much, they took it back to their state's societies. In time the tune became so popular, that within two years, it was copyrighted and adopted as the official song, of the C.A.R.

☆ A "Saving Old Ironsides" campaign was started. *The Constitution*, a U.S. frigate, first sailed in 1797, and gained fame in the War of 1812. During the war, cannonballs were bouncing off its side and the sailors said it must be made of iron. Of course, ships are made of wood, not iron, but the name stuck and we still refer to *The Constitution* as "Old Ironsides."

☆ Scholarships were awarded to two students at Tamassee DAR School in South Carolina.

☆ The restoration of Wakefield, the birthplace of George Washington is a current project. The society will help furnish the room representing the one in which George Washington was born.

☆ Inscription on staff of flag presented to the C.A.R.:

Presented to
NATIONAL SOCIETY C.A.R.
In Honor of
THE SESQUICENTENNIAL
of the Adoption of
THE FLAG OF U.S.A.
June 14, 1777
By The
COL. NICHOLAS RUXTON MOORE
SOCIETY, C.A.R.
State of Maryland
June 14, 1927

Washington's Birthplace, Wakefield, Virginia, where the C.A.R. will furnish his bedroom

☆ Indiana held its first Annual State Conference in Muncie on October 11, 1927 after having societies in the state for over thirty years!

☆ Texas and Virginia became State Societies.

☆ A Chair for DAR Constitution Hall was purchased by the Matthew Grant Society of Wichita, Kansas, in honor of our beloved National President.

☆ Miss Margaret Lothrop, daughter of the Founder of our Society, offered a prize of ten dollars for the best article of a Society meeting this year, the award to be made at the next Annual Convention.

☆ The Virginia Flag, presented to the National Society Children of the American Revolution by the Virginia Societies at the opening of the Annual Convention, April 17, 1928, was the first state flag ever presented to the C.A.R.

☆ A Resolution was adopted by the Thirty-seventh Continental Congress of the National Society Daughters of the American Revolution, April 1928. It reads:

> Whereas, We recognize in the Society of the Children of the American Revolution an organization devoted to the instruction of its membership in the fundamental principles of our Government as expressed in the Declaration of Independence and the Constitution of the United States, and to instilling into their minds

and hearts respect for governmental authority, obedience to law, love of our Country and its Flag, and devotion to the institutions of American liberty and patriotism; and

Whereas, Its objects and principles are the same as ours, and it is in every sense a training school for future loyal American Citizenship as well as for membership in our Society; now, therefore, be it

Resolved, That we, the Daughters of the American Revolution, in the Thirty-seventh Continental Congress assembled, go on record as heartily commending the Society of the Children of the American Revolution as being vital to the interests of our Organization, and to the future welfare of our Country; and we hereby urge our members to increase their efforts toward the creation and advancement of Children's Societies throughout the Country.

The NSSAR also endorsed the Children of the American Revolution.

☆ The C.A.R. Song was copyrighted in 1928 by Martha Parkinson Mills.

☆ A ceremony was held at the tomb of an Unknown Revolutionary Soldier, whose resting place was recently discovered in the historic burying ground of the Old Presbyterian Meeting House in Alexandria, Virginia.

On May 10, the National Board decided that the Society of the Children of the American Revolution would assume the obligation of erecting a suitable monument to the Unknown Soldier of the Revolutionary War, buried in the grounds of the Old Presbyterian Meeting House in Alexandria, Virginia.

☆ On June 9, an Oak tree in honor of the patriots of Lancaster County, Pennsylvania, who served in the Revolutionary War was presented to the Sixth Ward Memorial Park by the local C.A.R.

☆ "Wayside"—our founder's home became an historical memorial through the endeavors of Miss Margaret Lothrop and is opened to the public as another of Concord's literary shrines.

☆ The Cornerstone of Constitution Hall was laid October 30, 1928 and following is a list of articles placed in it by Mrs. Josiah A. Van Orsdel, National President, C.A.R.:

Photograph of Mrs. Harriett M. Lothrop, Founder of the National Society of the Children of the American Revolution.

Autographed photograph of Mrs. Josiah A. Van Orsdel, National President.

List of National Officers and State Directors.

Constitution and By-Laws of the National Society.

Story of the Origin of the Society.

Convention number of the Children's Magazine, 1928.

The C.A.R. Song with words and music

Official Ribbon.

Greetings to the Thirty-seventh Continental Congress of the National Society, Daughters of the American Revolution, by Mrs.

Josiah A. Van Orsdel, National President of National Society Children of the American Revolution, April sixteenth, 1928.

C.A.R. Creed.

☆ DAR Constitution Hall was erected as "a fitting memorial to that immortal document, the *Constitution of the United States.*" Constitution Hall contains the largest auditorium in the City with a seating capacity of 3,844; the National Headquarters of The Children of the American Revolution; the President General's Reception Rooms; Lobbies; and Lounges.

☆ November 12, 1928, under the auspices of the Sons of the American Revolution, exercises were held in Washington at the base of the statue of General Jose de San Martin, liberator of Argentina. The C.A.R. took part in the ceremony. In placing the beautiful wreath of large white chrysanthemums and white daisies, the National President said:

> "The members of the National Society of the Children of the American Revolution extend friendly greetings to the children of Argentina, and by the laying of this wreath express their admiration and reverence for the man whose life and noble deeds stand as an example to the youth of his country, and whose memory we have today assembled to honor."

☆ The Orange Dale Society, Orange, New Jersey, made scrapbooks which were presented to the children in the Orthopedic Hospital of Essex County at Christmas time.

☆ Oregon and Vermont became State Societies.

☆ A Charter was presented to the Rippowam Society, Stanford, Connecticut, at a meeting held February 23, 1929. The charter was framed in wood from an old elm tree planted by Oliver Ellsworth in Windsor, Connecticut, before the American Revolution.

☆ The Thirty-fourth Annual Convention opened in 1929 at the Red Cross Auditorium in Washington, D.C.

☆ Massachusetts and North Carolina state flags were presented to the National Society.

☆ Resolutions which were adopted at the Convention:

> Resolved, That the National Society of the Children of the American Revolution in convention assembled extend to the President General of the Daughters of the American Revolution their appreciation of her untiring efforts in behalf of the growth of their organization; her sympathetic interest in their programs and the lofty patriotic ideals set before them in all her public addresses will always remain an inspiration.

Whereas, There are sinister influences being used in schools to undermine the love of the flag and our country.

Be it Resolved, That the National Society, Children of the American Revolution, formulate a Bill and present to the United States Congress making it necessary for all teachers to subscribe to the oath of allegiance to our country before receiving a certificate to teach.

Whereas, The National Society of the Children of the American Revolution represent one of the largest and most important groups of youths in the nation.

Be it Resolved, That we pledge our allegiance to our country through our endeavor to help enforce all the laws of this nation.

The National Society, Children of the American Revolution, endorse House Office Bill No. 14, presented by the Hon. J. Charles Linthicum, to protect the *Star Spangled Banner* as the National Anthem of the United States of America.

Therefore, be it Resolved, That notice of this endorsed bill be sent to the State Directors and by them to all Presidents and Societies.

☆ The new National President, Mrs. Rhett Goode, was elected.

1929–1929

National President

Mrs. Rhett Goode
Mobile, Alabama

☆ National Project: Tomb of the Unknown Revolutionary Soldier in the graveyard of Old Presbyterian Meeting House, Alexandria, Virginia. Dedicated April 1929.

Tombs of unknown soldiers have been dedicated from many wars. A less famous tomb is that of the Unknown Soldier of the Revolutionary War. This is not, like that other Memorial, in Arlington National Cemetery but is situated in Alexandria, Virginia, in the churchyard of the Old Presbyterian Meeting House.

The inscription begins "Here lies a soldier hero of the Revolution, whose identity is known but to God—."

George Washington was a member of Christ Church in Alexandria but because the December weather made walking difficult along the then

The Tomb of the Unknown Soldier of the American Revolution in the graveyard of the Old Presbyterian Meeting House in Alexandria, Virginia

unpaved streets to Christ Church when he died in 1799, his memorial service was conducted at the Old Presbyterian Meeting House.

☆ Mrs. Herbert Hoover, wife of the President of the United States, received the members of the Children of the American Revolution at the White House.

☆ Society Activities

Members of Orange Dale Society, Orange, New Jersey, unveiled the marker to commemorate the planting of the first "Peace Tree" in New Jersey.

The Joseph Ormsby Society, Huron, South Dakota, dedicated a bronze marker on the site of the first public school in Huron and in Beadle County.

☆ New Jersey became a State Society.

☆ Mrs. Rhett Goode, National President, passed away suddenly on December 19, 1929 having served only eight months.

☆ Mrs. Percy Edwards Quin was elected to serve as National President.

1929–1931

National President

Mrs. Percy Edwards Quin
Natchez, Mississippi

☆ The Thirty-fifth Annual Convention was held in 1930 in the World War Memorial Building of the American Red Cross.

☆ A tree was planted on the grounds of Memorial Continental Hall in memory of Mrs. Rhett Goode, Past National President.

☆ To celebrate the 35th Anniversary of the C.A.R. the following was sent to all societies:

1895–1930
Thirty-Fifth Anniversary
April Fifth
Nineteen Hundred and Thirty
In Loving Remembrance of
Harriett M. Lothrop

Our Founder
The Board of Managers
of the
National Society of the Children
of the
American Revolution
desires all the Societies to hold a Birthday Party
with Cake, Candles and a Silver Tea Offering

☆ The Headquarters for our society will be at the Blackstone Hotel.

☆ One of the outstanding events of the Annual Convention was the placing of a molded stone in the fabric of Washington National Cathedral in memory of the late National President, Mrs. Rhett Goode, who died in Washington last winter. Mrs. Frederick T. Dubois, Honorary National President, placed the memorial stone.

Picture taken during the convention when a stone, giving by the Societies of the District of Columbia, was placed in the Washington National Cathedral in memory of our late National President, Mrs. Rhett Goode. Left to right are Mrs. Dubois, Past National President; Bishop Freeman; Rev. James E. Berkley; Mrs. Quin, National President; and Elwood A. Cobey, Jr.

☆ State flags from the following states were presented: Tennessee, Vermont, New York, Indiana, Missouri, Michigan, Connecticut, New Jersey, Kentucky, Georgia and California.

☆ National Projects included:

Harriett M. Lothrop Memorial Fund

Founder's Day Proceeds for the Building Fund

Wakefield Memorial Fund to help refurnish the room in which George Washington was born

Tamassee Scholarship Fund (the National Society is educating two girls at the school—Local Societies can help by contributing as little as one dollar each year)

Children of the American Revolution Magazine

Ellis Island Kindergarten Fund.

☆ William Dawes Society, Evanston, Illinois, planted a tree with the following inscription:

"Under the Washington Elm, Parent of this tree,
Washington first took command of the American
Army July 3, 1775. Presented by the William Dawes Society,
Children of the American Revolution."

☆ The Thirty-sixth Annual Convention was held in 1931 in the Auditorium of the Corcoran Gallery of Art, New York Avenue at 17th Street, N.W., Washington, D.C.

☆ The following state flags were presented: Nebraska, Pennsylvania, Texas, Ohio and Oklahoma.

☆ The new National President, Mrs. Samuel Shaw Arentz, was elected.

1931–1932

National President

Mrs. Samuel Shaw Arentz
Reno, Nevada

☆ California and Florida became State Societies.

☆ Nancy Hart Society, Bethlehem, Pennsylvania, marked the grave of Dr. Aquila Wilmot, the physician in attendance at the Revolutionary hospital in Bethlehem, in the old Moravian Cemetery on Market Street.

☆ Mrs. Eleanor Washington Howard, a descendant of the George Washington family and the last living person to be born at the first President's mansion, was guest of honor of the Children of the American Revolution, at a luncheon in the Shoreham Hotel, Saturday, in celebration of her seventh-fifth birthday anniversary.

☆ Mrs. Frederick T. Dubois, National President from 1905 to 1909, passed away August 17, 1931.

☆ On Labor Day, a tablet marking the site of Fort Ryerson was placed by the Ida Cummins Society, Waynesburg, Pennsylvania.

Washington's Kin Honored on Birthday. Left to right are: Mrs. John M. Kerr, cousin of Mrs. Howard; Mrs. Howard; Mrs. Samuel Shaw Arentz, wife of the Representative from Nevada and President of the Children of the American Revolution; and Mrs. Violet Blair Janin, first treasurer and oldest member of the Board of the C.A.R.

☆ The C.A.R. was honored to have a part in the Sesquicentennial of Cornwallis at Yorktown, Virginia, commemorating the realization of American Independence.

☆ The Thirty-seventh Annual Convention was held in Memorial Continental Hall in April 1932.

☆ The state flags of New Hampshire, Mississippi and South Dakota were presented. The N.S.C.A.R. insignia was placed in the Amphitheatre at Arlington Cemetery.

☆ The room furnished by the National society at Wakefield, Virginia, was dedicated.

☆ The N.S.C.A.R. accepted the offer of the S.A.R. of a silk C.A.R. Banner for annual competition. The banner is to be passed each year to the C.A.R. state organization that has transferred the largest number of members into the Society of the Sons of the American Revolution during the society year preceding the annual Congress. There will be a silver plate on the flag-staff on which each year the name of the winning state can be engraved.

☆ The Col. Thomas Hartley Society, York, Pennsylvania, presented a one act play entitled *George Washington's Birthday Party* to the DAR State Conference.

☆ Mrs. Herbert Hoover, wife of the President of the United States, invited the members to the White House.

☆ On December 5, 1932, Mrs. Arentz resigned as National President, and the National Board appointed Mrs. Josiah A. Van Orsdel, Honorary National President, to serve again. She served until 1933 when the new National President, Mrs. C. A. Swann Sinclair, was elected at the Thirty-eighth Annual Convention held in the Auditorium of the Red Cross Building.

1933–1937

National President

Mrs. C. A. Swann Sinclair
Alexandria, Virginia

☆ The Thirty-ninth through the Forty-second Annual Conventions were held in the Auditorium of the Red Cross Building.

☆ The Arkansas, Delaware and Florida state flags were presented.

☆ N.S.C.A.R. paid DAR $1.00 a year for use of business office room. The Harriett M. Lothrop Memorial Building Fund reached $4,856.25. The *Children of the American Revolution Magazine* was changed to five issues instead of six.

☆ Mrs. Franklin D. Roosevelt, wife of the President, received the C.A.R. in the East Room of the White House.

☆ The Nebraska state flag was presented to the Washington Memorial Chapel at Valley Forge, Pennsylvania, in the name of the State Society of the Children of the American Revolution of Nebraska.

☆ A ten-foot white oak tree was planted in the National Historical Grove and dedicated in the name of the National Society of the Children of the American Revolution.

☆ The *Children of the American Revolution Magazine* printed an issue in May 1933 as the Convention Number.

☆ The National society now has twenty-five state flags with the addition of Colorado, Illinois, and West Virginia.

☆ There was a tree planting, in Anacostia Park, D.C., by the C.A.R.

☆ It was decided to employ an accredited stenographer to take the minutes of the Tuesday and Wednesday sessions of the Annual Convention at a cost not to exceed $10.00 per day.

☆ The SAR Traveling Banner was first presented at the 1934 C.A.R. National Convention in the name of the National Society SAR. It was the personal gift of Mr. Thomas M. Williams of Orange, New Jersey, a member of the SAR Executive Committee. The Banner went to California for six months and to Oregon for the next six months since there was a tie.

☆ On October 18, 1934 the restoration of the Moore House in Yorktown, Virginia, which began in 1931 was formally dedicated.

☆ Mississippi and Arkansas became State Societies.

☆ A motion was adopted that N.S.C.A.R. start now, in its fortieth year, to set aside funds to be used for the purpose of a C.A.R. marker to be placed upon the graves of its departed National Presidents.

☆ The Bylaws were amended.

☆ Kansas and Maryland presented state flags and Kentucky became a State Society. The SAR Traveling Banner went to Oregon.

☆ The Oath of office to all newly elected officers was administered at Mt. Vernon.

☆ Mrs. Sinclair delivered the address at Yorktown for the celebration held in the garden of the Old Customhouse. C.A.R. members took part in the wreath laying at the Monument to Alliance and Victory.

☆ There was a C.A.R. Board Room plaque dedication:

Dedicated to the Memory of
MRS. DANIEL LOTHROP
Founder of the National Society
of the Children of the American
Revolution
April 5th, 1895
National President 1895-1901
Placed April 20, 1936

☆ The Honorable William Tyler Page, who wrote *The American's Creed,* attended the convention.

☆ Mrs. Franklin D. Roosevelt entertained the C.A.R. again at the White House.

☆ "Stunt Night" was an innovation. Visiting Societies are invited to put on a skit, not over five minutes in length with rehearsals held before the performance.

☆ Mrs. George M. Sternberg, National President 1901-1903, died in 1936.

☆ A new venture was introduced in the January 1937 issue of the *Children of the American Revolution Magazine* entitled *POST OFFICE DEPARTMENT BRANCH C.A.R.* The slogan of this new article was "Let's Get Acquainted." The goal was to use letters from C.A.R. members and Societies to get to know one another.

☆ A C.A.R. Ritual was published in the March 1937 issue of the *Children of the American Revolution Magazine* prepared by the Colonel John Neilson Society of New Brunswick, New Jersey.

☆ A silver Baptismal Ewer, in honor of Mrs. Eleanor Selden Washington Howard, National Vice President, was presented to Christ Church, Alexandria, Virginia, for her outstanding services to N.S.C.A.R. Mrs. Howard was born at Mt. Vernon, baptized in Christ Church Parish, and since 1892 has been a communicant of the church.

☆ Of interest is the following:

February 26, 1937

TO WHOM IT MAY CONCERN:

With my knowledge and consent, my Mother, Mrs. Eleanor Washington Howard, has presented to the National Society, Children of the American Revolution, her collection of Genealogical books and pamphlets. This collection is to be known as the Eleanor Washington Howard Collection and to be a part of the library of the National Society, Children of the American Revolution.

S/s Sarah H. Caldwell
Mrs. Hugh Caldwell

Witness:

s/s Frances M. Kerr
National Curator, N.S.C.A.R.

☆ The Forty-second Annual Convention was held in 1937 in the Auditorium of the National Red Cross Building.

☆ The National Chaplain prepared a booklet of programs, for use by the N.S.C.A.R., which sold for twenty-five cents.

☆ District of Columbia, Ohio, Rhode Island, and Nevada became State Societies. The state flag of South Carolina was presented.

☆ The C.A.R. members were received at the White House by Mrs. Franklin D. Roosevelt.

Mrs. Howard holding the little hood she wore during her days at Mt. Vernon

☆ The SAR Traveling Banner went to D.C. for six months and to New York for six months—again a tie.

☆ The Junior DAR presented a Traveling Banner to the National Society.

☆ Mrs. Eleanor Selden Washington Howard presented one of her childhood bonnets to the C.A.R. at its National Convention for permanent exhibit in its museum. It was discovered recently in the closet under the eaves where she used to do penance when naughty.

☆ The new National President, Mrs. William H. Pouch, was elected.

1937–1939

National President

Mrs. William H. Pouch
New York, New York

☆ In the summer of 1937, the Patriotic Education Committee was instigated.

☆ On August 16, 1937 the N.S.C.A.R. took part in the ceremonies of the laying of the cornerstone of the Theme Building of the New York World's Fair.

☆ Mrs. Pouch was the guest of honor at the first Annual Conference of the District of Columbia Society on October 15, 1937, and was instrumental in organizing the D.C. Society.

☆ DAR Continental Congress gave the N.S.C.A.R. permission to hold the Annual meeting in Memorial Continental Hall.

☆ Following is a notation from DAR minutes:

C.A.R. Building:

That permission be given to the C.A.R. Society to submit to the Executive Committee plans for building suitable administrative offices for the C.A.R. Society on the D.A.R. property.
(October 24-25, 1937 Executive Committee)

(Mrs. Pouch displayed suggestive plans for the proposed office quarters for the Children of the American Revolution.)
(October 24-25, 1937 Executive Committee)

That if and when the Children of the American Revolution Society has raised sufficient funds for a suitable building the National Society, Daughters of the American Revolution consider the advisability of allowing it to be placed on the D.A.R. property
(February 2, 1938 Board)

S/s Emily L. Currier
Recording Secretary General

November 26, 1951.

☆ Mrs. Eleanor Washington Howard, last of Washington's family to be born at Mt. Vernon, died in November, 1937, at the age of 81.

The Forty-third Annual Convention was held in Memorial Continental Hall.

☆ Mrs. Larz Anderson, Librarian-General, N.S.D.A.R., was an Honorary National Vice President of the C.A.R.

☆ The Constitution and Bylaws were revised.

☆ The SAR Traveling Banner went to Oregon and the DAR Junior Traveling Banner was presented to New York.

☆ The N.S.C.A.R. was represented at the SAR Congress in Dallas, Texas.

☆ The Patriotic Education Committee compiled, with the assistance of Naval Intelligence, Navy Department, a brief statement concerning the Revolutionary named ships which the C.A.R. National Society has been invited to sponsor. Only States recorded as of May 1, 1938, having held State Organization meetings were assigned ships:

Alabama — *Barry*	Florida — *Dolphin*
Arkansas — *Conynham*	Georgia — *Concord*
California — *Enterprise*	Illinois — *Hawk*
Colorado — *Nautilus*	Indiana — *Richmond*
Connecticut — *Ranger*	Kansas — *Gannet*
District of	Kentucky — *Beaver*
Columbia — *Stack*	Massachusetts — *Lexington*

70

Michigan — *Whipple*	Oregon — *Saratoga*
Mississippi — *Fanning*	Pennsylvania — *Humphries*
New Jersey — *Paul Jones*	Rhode Island — *Hopkins*
New York — *New York*	South Dakota — *Porpoise*
North Carolina — *Raleigh*	Texas — *Wasp*
Ohio — *Phoenix*	Vermont — *Truxton*
Oklahoma — *O'Brien*	Virginia — *Yorktown*

The names given to ships of the early Navy honored generally the colony or town in which they were obtained or built, the patriot who assisted in outfitting them, or contemporary leaders and events.

Memorial Lights
"Beautiful Stars of Memory"

MAY PERPETUAL LIGHT SHINE
UPON THE CHILDREN OF
TAMASSEE
PLACED IN MEMORY OF
HELEN POUCH
WHO ENTERED INTO LIGHT ETERNAL
JANUARY 9 1919
BY MARY BREWSTER LOCKWOOD

Tamassee DAR School
Tamassee, South Carolina 29686

The first four Memorial Lights at Tamassee DAR School were dedicated between 1933 - 1936. Later, one was given in memory of Helen Pouch, daughter of our Beloved "Aunt Helena." Also, there is an avenue of Memorial Trees and one was given in honor of Mrs. C.A. Swann Sinclair, Honorary National President, N.S.C.A.R.

☆ Mrs. John Morrison Kerr, the incoming National President, and another lady launched a campaign to get a District of Columbia flag. Mrs. Kerr suggested that the flag should include the stripes from the Washington Family coat of arms. On June 16, 1938, Congress created a commission to procure a design for a D.C. flag and it is the one seen today.

☆ On October 11, 1938, Shirley Temple, the famous child movie star, was made the first National Associate Member of the National Society, Children of the American Revolution.

☆ The Stamp Column was started in the November 1938 *Children of the American Revolution Magazine* by Grahame T. Smallwood, Jr.

☆ Kansas, North Carolina, Oklahoma, Pennsylvania, Tennessee, West Virginia and Wisconsin all became State Societies.

☆ It was recommended that on Founders' Day one of the scholarships at Tamassee be designated the Harriett M. Lothrop Scholarship. The price of the *Children of the American Revolution Magazine* was raised from ten to fifteen cents.

Mrs. William H. Pouch with Shirley Temple in her bungalow at the Twentieth Century-Fox Studios in Hollywood, California

☆ The DAR Traveling Banner was first presented at the 1939 National Convention by Mrs. William H. Pouch in the name of the Junior Membership Committee, NSDAR.

☆ The National Board of Management authorized Newman Bros., Inc. of Cincinnati, Ohio, to furnish C.A.R. grave markers for our members who have entered "Life Eternal."

☆ At this time there were 29 organized State Societies with Junior State Presidents.

☆ N.S.C.A.R. voted to restore and furnish the smallest of the bedrooms in Gadsby's Tavern in Alexandria, Virginia, in honor of the Honorary National President, Mrs. C. A. Swann Sinclair. The Northern Virginia Societies restored the middle bedroom in honor of the National President, Mrs. William H. Pouch.

☆ The following resolutions were presented:

> WHEREAS, It is desirable that the members of the C.A.R. have a knowledge and understanding of the actual work of the National Officers, therefore,
>
> RESOLVED, That the National Board be and are hereby authorized to appoint Junior Officers to correspond with the National Officers.
>
> The presentation of a Resolution to the Resolution Committee by Mrs. Howard R. Arnest, relative to the placing of the Indian School, Chemawa, situated near Salem, Oregon, on the list of Approved Indian Schools of the C.A.R. brought forth the following resolution which was adopted by the Convention. Move to refer to Approved School Committee for their consideration and with power to act if in their judgment the school meets the requirements of our rules.

☆ During the afternoon session of the 44th Annual Convention in 1939, the National President, Mrs. Pouch, presented H. Brooks Gardner who served as Presiding Officer pro tem. After opening exercises, Lyons Mills Howland, Junior State President of Michigan, took the chair as President Officer of the afternoon session.

Lyons Howland brought the following greetings:

> "To the National Society Children of the American Revolution go my heartiest and sincerest greetings.
>
> "As we enter another C.A.R. year, the one great prayer that I might have is that, inspired by Almighty God and by the wonderful accomplishments of our own "Aunt Helen," the new C.A.R. Administration, headed by Mrs. John Morrison Kerr, will carry on the glorious banner of Americanism and do great and greater things in its magnificent

work of training young America to live up to the high ideals and standards set up by our inspired forefathers.

"And so, my greetings straight from the heart to C.A.R., and long may it live."

Mrs. Pouch expressed her pleasure at the manner in which the Junior organization conducted the meeting and desired to see in the future an active Junior organization with the National Officers as advisors.

☆ The SAR Traveling Banner went to New York and the Junior DAR Banner to Pennsylvania.

☆ The new National President, Mrs. John Morrison Kerr, was elected.

1939–1941

Junior National President

Lyons Mills Howland
Highland Park, Michigan

National President

Mrs. John Morrison Kerr
Washington, D.C.

☆ On May 20, 1939, National President, Mrs. John Morrison Kerr, had the honor of announcing the appointment of Lyons Mills Howland, of Michigan, as the first Junior National President.

☆ The New York World's Fair made August 7, 1939 a special day for Patriotic Societies and the C.A.R. participated.

☆ Illinois and Maine became State Societies. Rhode Island and the District of Columbia presented state flags.

☆ States were divided into nine divisions with a National Vice President assigned to each: Northern, Northeastern, Eastern, Southeastern, Central, West Central, Southern, Western and Pacific. There are now thirty-three states that have State Organizations.

☆ A movie was produced by Columbia Pictures called *Five Little Peppers and How They Grew* starring Edith Fellows and Dorothy Peterson. This charming picture closely followed the story by Margaret Sidney (Harriett Lothrop), beloved by at least two generations.

☆ Mrs. Frank W. Mondell, National President from 1919 to 1925, passed away November 7, 1939.

☆ In December, the Building Fund reached $14,343.83.

☆ In February 1940 former President Herbert Hoover invited the C.A.R. to serve on his committee for Finnish Relief.

☆ At the Forty-fifth Annual Convention Lyons Howland made the following remarks:

> "We, the members of the first Junior National Board in the history of the Children of the American Revolution salute you!
>
> "For a long time preparations were being made for the launching of this plan and we are doubly happy for this action: first, that the Senior Board felt that the time was ripe at last and second, that we were thus so highly honored. And so, entering this new era of C.A.R. work, we must realize that, no matter how gay and carefree are our duties and contacts, there is an underlying and serious responsibility resting on our shoulders. We must realize that, in these alarmingly uncertain days, it is more important than ever before for The Children of the American Revolution to carry the banner of Americanism; that, in these heartsick, strife-torn times, America must keep her head and we must be determined that above all, 'this nation under God shall have a new birth of freedom that government of the people, by the people and for the people shall not perish from the earth.'"

☆ Junior National Officers were permitted to wear the official ribbon around the neck with C.A.R. Insignia suspended therefrom.

☆ It was decided to adopt the official N.S.C.A.R. insignia as an emblem to be worn on an arm band by members of the C.A.R. on suitable occasions and twenty such arm bands were ordered.

☆ A resolution was adopted that all contributions for the Aesop's Fable Mantel in Kenmore at Fredericksburg, Virginia, be placed in an endowment fund. This was a state project of the C.A.R.

☆ The National Board authorized the use of State Chairmen's Pins.

☆ Alabama, Maryland, Minnesota, Canal Zone/Panama and Utah became State Societies.

☆ The first memorial forest planted in New Mexico was named "The New Mexico C.A.R. Memorial Forest." It was established, April 1940, in the Aspen Basin, about eighteen miles from Santa Fe.

☆ June 15, 1940 was designated *C.A.R. Day* at the New York World's Fair.

*New Mexico
C.A.R. Memorial
Forest
Area No. 1—
Established
April 1940*

☆ In the early part of 1941 the C.A.R. member National Board adopted a resolution that every State C.A.R. Society would contribute ten cents per member toward the continuation of the restoration of Moore House.

☆ Mrs. William H. Pouch, Honorary National President, N.S.C.A.R., became President General of the Daughters of the American Revolution.

☆ Alabama and Minnesota state flags were presented.

☆ The motion to adopt pins for junior national officers was adopted. The President's pin will be passed on to his successor.

C.A.R. Day at the World's Fair. Bobby Lee Williamson (in costume) reciting The American's Creed, H. Brooks Gardner, presiding

Coupons to be used for Admission to Attractions at The World's Fair of 1940 in New York City on the National Society Children of the American Revolution Day June 15, 1940

☆ The Forty-sixth Annual Convention was held in Memorial Continental Hall April 18-21, 1941.

☆ The SAR Traveling Banner went to Connecticut and the Junior DAR to New York.

☆ William S. Berner was elected the new Junior National President and the Junior Officers were installed at Mt. Vernon.

☆ Mrs. Louise Moseley Heaton was installed as the National President.

1941–1945

Junior National President	National President
1941 – 1943	1941 – 1945

William S. Berner
East Orange, New Jersey

Mrs. Louise Moseley Heaton
Clarksdale, Mississippi

☆ The sum of $200.00 for the use of the National President for travel-ing was approved. A committee was appointed to prepare a set of Junior National Bylaws.

☆ Delaware and New Mexico became State Societies and Wyoming state flag was presented. The SAR Traveling Banner went to the District of Columbia and the DAR Traveling Banner to New Jersey.

☆ The funds that were collected for the continuing restoration of Moore House, the FIRST C.A.R. NATIONAL PROJECT PROPOSED BY THE MEMBERS, were used to purchase articles to furnish the Children's Room, a small room which adjoins the room where legend says the documents of surrender of Cornwallis to Washington were actually prepared. Known today as the Family Parlor, the room also contains authentic period pieces given in honor of, or by Seniors. The project resulted in a total of $1,296.21 being raised from a majority of the State Societies.

The Dedication of the Family Parlor was held October 19, 1941. William S. Berner, the first elected National President, N.S.C.A.R., presented the following remarks:

> "We are once again side by side with the Daughters of the American Revolution for our Children's Room is connecting with the beautiful room that the Daughters restored some years ago. May we never be further apart! Every C.A.R. member had a part in the work of this room and it makes me happy to know that it has been done this way. You will remember that it was the surrender of Cornwallis to Washington which took place in this house that brought it fame. That surrender signifies the preservation of our American way of life. We of the C.A.R. are happy to be able to help preserve this room so that thousands of Americans may receive the same inspiration of freedom and liberty from visiting the room that we received by giving our dimes for its restoration."

☆ The C.A.R. Headquarters Building Fund and the Harriett M. Lothrop Fund totaled $15,647.40.

☆ In February of 1942 the National Board voted to cancel the Forty- seventh Annual Convention due to war conditions and the housing problem.[3]

☆ The C.A.R. Headquarters had the 4' × 6' C.A.R. Flag, in all its five colors, from Annin & Company, New York, available for purchase. The National President accepted the invitation to serve on the National Council of '76 which sponsored the Nation-wide observance of Flag Week.

☆ Mrs. Franklin D. Roosevelt received the members at the White House.

☆ The C.A.R. members were very active during the war period collecting money for various uses. A bed was given to the Children's Hospital in Washington, D.C., and an ambulance was given to the Red Cross for use on Staten Island. The C.A.R. Society in Thomasville, North Carolina, pooled their money and purchased an ambulance for the War Department. A check for $2,000 for a club mobile was presented to Miss Mabel T. Boardman, Secretary of the American Red Cross. The C.A.R. was prominent in the sale of War Bonds and stamps. An amphibious ship, LCL617, was sponsored by the society.

☆ The SAR Traveling Banner went to New York while the DAR Traveling Banner had a tie between New Jersey and New York.

[3]The Japanese attacked Pearl Harbor in Hawaii on December 5, 1941, which forced the United States into World War II.

★ On February 4, 1943, the National Board voted that due to war conditions the 1943-1944 Annual Convention would not be held. During this period, Robert Rooe Simpson served as Junior National President.

Junior National President
1943 – 1945

Robert Rooe Simpson
Indianapolis, Indiana

★ New Hampshire became a State Society. The SAR Traveling Banner went to New York and the DAR Traveling Banner went to Pennsylvania.

★ The C.A.R. Board Room was released for the use of the National Red Cross Society personnel for the operation of the Committee of Service for Prisoners of War.

★ The October Board meeting voted to hold the 1944-1945 Annual Convention on April 22 at the Hotel Commodore in New York City.

★ Over $1,500 in War Bonds went to the War Department for a Jeep for the Armed Forces.

★ The C.A.R. Grandmothers' Club knitted afghans for the Army, Navy and Marine hospitals.

★ Mrs. Percy Edwards Quin, National President from 1929 to 1931, passed away in November of 1943.

Children Present Jeep to Army. Lieutenant Samuel Corcoran receives a jeep christened "The Spirit of '76" from the Children of the American Revolution members. Left to right: Mary Allene Farnsworth, Lieutenant Corcoran, John Eagleton, Mrs. Louise Moseley Heaton and Mrs. Donald B. Adams

☆ The Forty-ninth Annual Convention was held in New York City.

☆ The SAR Traveling Banner went to New York and Connecticut and the DAR Traveling Banner to Pennsylvania. The Wyoming state flag was presented.

☆ The DAR chapters of the greater New York area united to sponsor the ships' crews of four Landing Crafts Infantry. The project was so successful that the National Society was asked by the Amphibious Forces to undertake a mass sponsoring of ships by the State Societies, the District of Columbia and by the Children of the American Revolution.

☆ D.C.C.A.R. members presented a portable piano to the National Naval Medical Center. It was mounted on a platform with rubber wheels to facilitate movement from ward to ward.

☆ A Treasury Testimony of Merit was presented to the N.S.C.A.R. for credit given for the purchase of over $1,800,000.00 of War Bonds designated for the purchase of a bomber.

☆ Mrs. C. A. Swann Sinclair, National President from May 1933 to 1937, passed away on January 22, 1945.

☆ Plans were made to have a National Officers Club for the C.A.R. Society. Mrs. C. A. Swann Sinclair was named Founder and Honorary President of the Club. Mrs. William H Pouch, Honorary National President, was appointed the first President.

☆ The new Junior National President, Virginia Simons, and the National President, Mrs. Reuben Edward Knight were elected and installed.

1945–1947

50TH ANNIVERSARY

Junior National President

National President

Virginia Frances Simons
Washington, D.C.

Mrs. Reuben Edward Knight
Alliance, Nebraska

☆ The 50th Anniversary of the C.A.R. could not be celebrated because of the war.

☆ The C.A.R. 50th Anniversary War Project to adopt 6 children in war torn countries (Holland, France, Italy, Belgium, Germany and China) for a period of one year as part of the Foster Parents' Plan.

☆ The National Project was playgrounds for Tamassee and Kate Duncan Smith DAR Schools in memory of Mrs. C. A. Swann Sinclair, Honorary National President.

☆ A garden tea, in observance of our 50th year, was held at the home of Mrs. Robert V. H. Duncan, who later became President General, NSDAR.

☆ The Senior National Officers' Club was organized May 10, 1946, in Washington, D.C., with fifty-one Charter Members attending. The late Mrs. C. A. Swann Sinclair, Honorary Senior National President, N.S.C.A.R., promoted the organization to further the objects of the National Society of the Children of the American Revolution, to assist in giving continuity in the work of the national committees, to foster cooperation among the Senior National Officers and to be of friendly assistance to new Senior Officers.

Any member of the DAR, SAR or S.R. having served as a Senior National Officer, Senior State Director or Senior State President or as a National Officer or State President of the National Society of the Children of the American Revolution is eligible to Membership in this Club. The

The Bell Tower next to the Washington Memorial Chapel at Valley Forge, Pennsylvania

Senior National Officers' Club operates as a separate entity from the National Society C.A.R.

☆ The Annual Convention was restored May 11, 1946 in Memorial Continental Hall.

☆ The September 1946 Issue No. 4 of the *Children of the American Revolution Magazine* was named *Information Edition*.

☆ Over $2,000 was sent to Kate Duncan Smith and Tamassee DAR Schools, part for playground equipment and the rest for additional acres to be cultivated by the children.

☆ A plaque was placed on a stone at the base of the Valley Forge Memorial Bell Tower in Pennsylvania honoring the C.A.R. for providing the frieze of carved native animals and birds at the top of the Memorial Room.

☆ The Fifty-second Annual Convention was held in Memorial Continental Hall.

☆ South Carolina became a State Society. Maine presented a state flag,

☆ The SAR Traveling Banner went to New York and so did the DAR Traveling Banner.

☆ The Junior National President, Patricia Edwards, and the National President, Mrs. Donald Bennett Adams, were elected and installed.

1947–1951

National President	Junior National President
1947 – 1951	1947 – 1949
Mrs. Donald Bennett Adams	**Patricia Edwards**
New Rochelle, New York	*Grand Rapids, Michigan*

☆ The Junior National Project was a Permanent Honor Roll of those men and women who served the nation in the past wars placed at the Patriots' Transept of the Washington National Cathedral in Washington, D.C.

✮ The following is a quotation from an article entitled *OUR NEW BUILD-ING* by Mrs. V. Eugene Holcombe, Chairman, Building Promotion Committee, Daughters of the American Revolution:

> "Patience is a rare virtue but it brings its own reward. For years the C.A.R. has demonstrated patience. Without complaint it has carried forward its splendid work from cramped and inadequate quarters in the Administration Building of the D.A.R. The marvel of it is that the C.A.R. has been able to function at all under such handicaps.
>
> "Under the new building expansion program, the C.A.R. will be provided with larger quarters fully equipped to take care of the expanding growth of the Society.
>
> "One of the main reasons for undertaking the $900,000 new Building Project was to provide added space for the C.A.R. Therefore, plans have been made to move C.A.R. National Headquarters into the space now occupied by the D.A.R. Library. It gives me the deepest satisfaction, therefore, to make this announcement because for many years the activities of the N.S.C.A.R. have been close to my heart."

✮ The Massachusetts C.A.R. Society presented a bronze marker at the grave of our Founder, Mrs. Daniel Lothrop.

✮ The Fifty-third Annual Convention was held in Memorial Continental Hall.

✮ Cuba and Washington became State Societies and presented state flags.

✮ The SAR and DAR Traveling Banners both went to New York.

✮ Grahame T. Smallwood, Jr., of Washington, D.C., was made an Honorary Junior National Vice President for life.

✮ A marker was placed at Kenmore, home of Betty Washington Lewis and Colonel Fielding Lewis, Fredericksburg, Virginia, in front of the Aesop's Mantel endowed by the C.A.R.

✮ For the first time since 1941, Yorktown Day at Yorktown, Virginia, took on the semblance of a pre-war celebration on October 19, 1947. It was the 25th ceremony sponsored by the Comte de Grasse Chapter, DAR. Mrs. John Morrison Kerr, Honorary National President, N.S.C.A.R., and Mrs. Pouch, who presented an inspiring address, were among the participants.

✮ The C.A.R. museum will be in the north wing of the present DAR Library, which is to be our permanent Headquarters, when the DAR Building plan is completed.

✮ C.A.R. Members Slogan for 1948—EACH A NEW MEMBER

✮ Mrs. Harry S. Truman, wife of the President, received the C.A.R. at a White House reception.

☆ The *Children of the American Revolution Magazine* was increased from 50 cents to $1.00 per year.

☆ Following is a copy of a DAR Ruling pertaining to C.A.R.:

RULINGS OF NATIONAL BOARD OF MANAGEMENT
NATIONAL SOCIETY, DAUGHTERS OF THE AMERICAN REVOLUTION

April 24, 1948

That the National Society of the Children of the American Revolution be granted permanent headquarters in the north wing, now occupied by the library, alterations for same to be made at their expense and according to their plans.

> S/s Maymie D. Lammers
> Recording Secretary General
> N.S.D.A.R.

Delivered to:
National Society, Children of the American Revolution
April 28, 1948.

☆ This year, for the first time, the C.A.R. had a page in the DAR Brochure which went to every DAR Chapter.

☆ Authorization was given by the National Board for the wearing of C.A.R. ribbon as a service bar along with other ribbons worn by members in the Armed Forces.

☆ A traveling fund was established for the Junior National President.

☆ A term of five years was approved for the Honorary National Vice Presidents to serve.

☆ *The C.A.R. Song* was transposed to a lower key, which may be more difficult to play, but will be much easier to sing.

☆ Dedication of the C.A.R. Tree at Memorial Continental Hall on the north corner, opposite the one planted in 1920, for the Children of the American Revolution who served in World War II, took place.

☆ The C.A.R. Insignia. in red, blue and gold was approved to be used as a seal sticker. When a copy of the Official Insignia is used as a sticker, it shall be used at the top or upper left hand corner. It is not to be used as a fastener for holding paper together. Common uses of the sticker are program covers, yearbook covers and scrapbook cover sheets. The stickers were ready for sale from the C.A.R. National Headquarters and come in two sizes: 1¼ inch in diameter and 2½ inch in diameter. The stickers cost of two cents each for the small size and five cents each for the large size.

A copy of the Official Insignia cannot be used for any other purpose unless specifically authorized by the Senior National Board of Management. A letter giving full details must be sent to the National President, N.S.C.A.R., BEFORE proceeding.

☆ Staff Party—On the evening of October 20, 1948, a Card Party was held in the corridors of Constitution Hall by the Office Staffs of the C.A.R. and DAR for the benefit of the DAR Building Fund. They realized over the $2,200.00 which was the goal and are purchasing one of the new elevators called for in the building plans. Nearly all of the members of the C.A.R. Board who attended the Board Meeting stayed over for the party and "a good time was had by all."

☆ The DAR grew from a membership in 1902 of 38,006 to an all- inclusive 380,420 in 1948; fifteen Presidents General came and went. Approximately 63,000 Children of the American Revolution grew up to become members of the DAR and SAR by 1948.

☆ The new Junior National President, Edward Benjamin Dake, was elected and installed

Junior National President
1949 – 1950

Edward Benjamin Dake
Parkersburg, West Virginia

☆ The Fifty-fourth and Fifty-fifth Annual Conventions were held in the Ballroom of the Mayflower Hotel, Washington, D.C.

☆ Louisiana became a State Society.

☆ Mrs. Estella Armstrong O'Bryne, President General, NSDAR, 1947-1950, remarked that the greatest achievement of her administration is one that provides lasting tribute: the erection of the three-story addition to the Administration Building, part of the National Headquarters complex. During this period, the auditorium in Memorial Continental Hall was remodeled into the DAR Library. The old Library, on the second floor of Constitution Hall, was converted into National Headquarters for the National Society Children of the American Revolution and a meeting room for the DAR National Officers Club.

☆ Dedication of the C.A.R. Mississippi State Society room at Rosalie, the antebellum home owned by the Mississippi State Society DAR at Natchez, Mississippi, which was restored in memory of the late Mrs. Percy Edwards Quin, Past National President, C.A.R.

☆ $9,000 was paid to the DAR Building Fund for the C.A.R. National Headquarters. This was money which had been collected for a C.A.R.

Building Fund ever since Mrs. Lothrop, our founder, was National President.

☆ Dedication of the new Headquarters of the C.A.R. took place on Friday morning, April 21, 1950, at 9 o'clock. Mrs. Donald Bennett Adams, National President, dedicated the Headquarters in the memory of Harriett M. Lothrop, our Founder.

CONTRACT FOR USE OF OFFICE SPACE

THIS CONTRACT Made and entered into by and between the NATIONAL SOCIETY, THE DAUGHTERS OF THE AMERICAN REVOLUTION, party of the first part, and NATIONAL SOCIETY CHILDREN OF THE AMERICAN REVOLUTION, party of the second part,

WITNESSETH:

Party of the first part hereby gives to the party of the second part the use of the south end of the old library in Constitution Hall, being approximately two-thirds of said room for permanent headquarters, such space having dimensions of approximately 18 feet by 78 feet at one end thereof and 35 feet by 49 feet at the other end thereof.

Party of the second part agrees to pay in advance for the maintenance of the above space the sum of Two Hundred Dollars ($200) per year, payable semi-annually on May 1st and November 1st of each year and $25.00 per year for electricity payable in advance May 1st.

Party of the second part further agrees that all alterations, redecorating and repairs required in the use of the above space shall be at the expense of the party of the second part so long as this contract exists.

No structural changes shall be made except by the approval of the Executive Committee of the party of the first part.

IN WITNESS WHEREOF parties hereto have executed this Agreement by their proper officers, this 18th day of April 1950.

NATIONAL SOCIETY OF THE DAUGHTERS
OF THE AMERICAN REVOLUTION

Witness:

By *Estella A. O'Byrne*
Pres. Gen.

NATIONAL SOCIETY OF THE CHILDREN OF THE
AMERICAN REVOLUTION

Laura E. Cooß

Frances Washington Kerr By *Helen B. Adams*
Nat. Pres.

April 18, 1950 Contract For Use Of Office Space

☆ Upon the resignation of Edward Benjamin Dake, Daniel Stuart Pope, III, was elected and installed to serve as Junior National President.

Junior National President
1950 – 1951

Daniel Stuart Pope, III
New Haven, Connecticut

☆ National Project of the Mountain Schools Committee: Piano for Tamassee DAR School. Special Project: Our Museum needs "Heirlooms" dated prior to 1825.
☆ Ten display cases were given to the C.A.R. Museum by the DAR.
☆ A quote from a message to our Annual Convention from Mrs. James B. Patton, President General, NSDAR, on April 22, 1950:

> "It is a great pleasure to know that I am, personally, going to be associated even closer with the Children of the American Revolution. It is fine that our offices of the Daughters of the American Revolution and the Children of the American Revolution are so close together, and that we may cooperate with each other more and more.
>
> "The Daughters of the American Revolution need you and you certainly need the Daughters of the American Revolution. You need the wisdom of the older people. We need the imagination and the enthusiasm of the young people."

☆ When the C.A.R. moved into its present quarters, the Library-Museum became an active and important part of its program. Here are two examples of some of the items.

FOUNDER'S ALCOVE

In this alcove are grouped pictures of Mrs. Daniel Lothrop, founder of the Children of the American Revolution, copies of books she wrote under the pen name of Margaret Sidney, her membership pins in patriotic societies, and her Founder's Pin of C.A.R. with the familiar emblem super-imposed on a sunburst hanging from the officer's pin.

'TWAS THE 18th OF APRIL IN '75

A pair of pierced tin lanterns such as were used to signal Paul Revere. A block of wood from the original "belfry tower of the old North Church" and a small copy of Cyrus Dallin's statue of Paul Revere on his famous midnight ride.

☆ A Junior Magazine Chairman was appointed by the National President. The Editor of the *Children of the American Revolution Magazine* was invited to attend the 16th International Children's Christmas Broadcast.

☆ C.A.R. contributions to the NSDAR Building Fund are now over $9,400.00.

☆ The Fifty-sixth Annual Convention was held in the Ballroom of the Mayflower Hotel in Washington, D.C.

☆ The Junior National President, Caroline Thwing Brown, and the National President, Mrs. Charles Carroll Haig, were elected and installed.

1951–1955

Junior National President	National President
1951 – 1952	1951 – 1955
Caroline Thwing Brown	Mrs. Charles Carroll Haig
Bethesda, Maryland	*Washington, D.C.*

☆ The first Regional Meeting of the Southeastern States was held in Birmingham, Alabama, on August 16, 1951.

☆ Mrs. Raymond C. Goodfellow, National Chaplain, was thanked for her generous gift of Hymnals presented to the Children's Chapel of the Washington National Cathedral in the name of the C.A.R.

☆ On October 19, 1951, the N.S.C.A.R. participated in the Yorktown Day Celebration. A marker was unveiled for the room at Moore House furnished by the National Society.

☆ In December 1951, the establishment of the Permanent Fund was approved by the National Board of Management.

☆ On December 21, 1951, Mrs. Josiah A. Van Orsdel of Beatrice, Nebraska, passed away. She served as National President, C.A.R., from 1925 to 1929 and 1932 to 1933.

☆ Through the interest and generosity consisting of SAR members, the National Advisory Committee underwrote the cost of printing a *C.A.R. Handbook*.

☆ A quilt was presented to the C.A.R. Museum by Mrs. Cornell Cree, State President of New Jersey.

☆ Clarence W. Chachere, III, of New Orleans, Louisiana, won the Magazine Cover design contest.

☆ A second bedroom in Gadsby's Tavern dedicated to "Aunt Helen" Pouch was refurnished as a National Project.

☆ Miss Jean Jacobs became the Executive Secretary for the C.A.R.

☆ The Fifty-seventh through the Sixtieth Annual Conventions were all held in the Ballroom of the Mayflower Hotel in Washington, D.C.

☆ Mrs. Harry S. Truman, wife of the President, entertained the members in the White House.

☆ Before the opening of the C.A.R. Annual Convention, the DAR had its Continental Congress and adopted the following resolution:

"Children of the American Revolution

Whereas, The conflict between the principles of our Republic and the doctrines of totalitarianism is growing in strength and tenacity, thereby with ever increasing insistence, threatening the future of the youth of today; and

Whereas, The Society of the Children of the American Revolution is devoted to the instruction of its members in the fundamental principles of our government, respect for Constitutional authority, obedience to law, and devotion to the United States of America and its Flag.

Resolved, That the members of the National Society, Daughters of the American Revolution be urged to show increased interest in the Society of the Children of the American Revolution who are naturally entitled to be cherished as the special charges and dearest wards of the parent-society."

☆ The incoming Junior National President, Robert Allan Watson, was elected and installed.

Junior National President
1952 – 1953

Robert Allan Watson
Fort Worth, Texas

☆ The National Project was for three schools: Tamassee DAR School—
a large electric range for the kitchen and the C.A.R. Walk;

Kate Duncan Smith DAR School—a large power mower for the lawns; and

Crossnore—bedspreads.

☆ In June of 1952, there was a presentation of two large floor cases to the museum from the D.C. Home Makers Committee of 1944-1946.

☆ The first Regional Meeting of the Mid-Western States was in August.

☆ The First Lady, Mrs. Dwight D. Eisenhower, received the members at the White House.

☆ The incoming Junior National President, Cornelia Brandon Cabral, was elected and installed.

Junior National President
1953 – 1954

Cornelia Brandon Cabral
New Orleans, Louisiana

☆ The National Project was to raise $2200 to purchase a tractor and plow for Bacone Indian College in Muskogee, Oklahoma.

☆ On July 4th the C.A.R. wreath was laid at the tomb of General de Lafayette in the Cimetiere de Picpus, Paris, France.

☆ The Honorable David Lynn, Architect of the Capitol, gave a set of six beautiful walnut boards, each 9″ by 40″ × 1″ taken from the halls of Congress, dating back almost to the American Revolution. A scroll with the names of Junior and Senior Presidents from 1895 to 1995 will be placed on the boards.

☆ On April 22, 1954, the Senior National Board of Management ruled that N.S.C.A.R. would participate in the annual observance of the Surrender at Yorktown as a member of the Yorktown Day Association. Full membership was granted by the Association on May 21, 1953.

☆ The SAR Traveling Banner went to New York and the DAR Traveling Banner went to New Jersey.

☆ The members took a trip to the White House.

☆ The incoming Junior National President, Laurence A. Stith, Jr., was elected and installed.

Junior National President
1954 – 1955

Laurence A. Stith, Jr.
New Bern, North Carolina

☆ The National Project was for the mountain schools: Crossnore—electric organ for Chapel; Tamassee DAR School—electric meat saw; Kate Duncan Smith DAR School—new silo for storage of grain.

☆ A Freedoms Foundation Medal was engraved: For Outstanding Achievement in Bringing About a Better Understanding of the American Way of Life was awarded to the Priscilla Alden Society of Temple, Texas, for its "Flag Etiquette Program."

☆ The case for the Kathleen Douglass Memorial Collection of Dolls was installed and paid for by gifts from the members.

☆ The first National Merit Award for the Most Outstanding Society in the Nation was awarded to the Lydia Darrach Society, Santa Monica, California.

☆ The first Regional Meeting of the Eastern States was in August 1954.

☆ A new National Committee was authorized by the 63rd Continental Congress, NSDAR, for cooperation with the Children of the American Revolution and our own Mrs. Charles Carroll Haig became the first National Chairman. Following is partial quote from her letter to the State Chairmen:

"It is a real pleasure to greet you as National Chairman of the new D.A.R. National Committee on C.A.R. Work. The Senior Leaders are very grateful to the National Society Daughters of the American Revolution for the action of its 63rd Continental Congress in creating this National Committee on C.A.R. Work. It is hoped that it will mean a closer relationship with D.A.R. and trust it will bring about a keener interest of D.A.R. members in the programs and activities of this Society which membership is the young people of the Daughters and Sons of the American Revolution. The C.A.R. leaders need your interest and encouragement.

"Those states which have had a State C.A.R. Committee set-up will now be a part of the National Committee. The other states will, we hope, become a part in the appointment of a State Chairman and Chapter Chairmen.

"Each of us as members of the D.A.R. has a serious responsibility to our OWN youth as the moral fibre of our citizens of tomorrow depends on us. It is important we bring our young people into an organization such as C.A.R. before they form attachments which are alien in thought to our principles. Let us not lose our youth to other youth organizations.

"With deep gratitude in my heart for the interest and cooperation of D.A.R. members and with a sincere prayer that through this new Committee on C.A.R. Work more of our young people will be encouraged to join the C.A.R. and receive the fine patriotic training offered through its effective programs."

☆ The D.A.R. Honor Roll requirements for 1954-1955 reads: "Did your Chapter work for at least NINE National Committees, other than those listed above? Namely: American Indians, American Music, American Red Cross, Americanism, C.A.R., etc." This has been a great help in securing financial support for the C.A.R. which might not have been previously donated.

☆ The incoming Junior National President, Lillian Diane Weller, and National President, Mrs. E. Stewart James, were elected and installed.

☆ The Vice President of the United States, Richard M. Nixon, greeted Miss Weller and Mrs. James in his offices following the 1955 Convention.

1955–1958

Junior National President 1955 – 1956	National President 1955 – 1958

Lillian Diane Weller *Long Beach, California*	**Mrs. E. Stewart James** *Gloucester, Virginia*

☆ A Maintenance Fund was established for the upkeep of the Sinclair and Pouch Honorarium Rooms at Gadsby's Tavern.

☆ The National Project was again for the schools: St. Mary's School for Indian Girls—30 desks, 16 dressers and chairs, and 6 irons; Tamassee—30 gallon kettle; Kate Duncan Smith—electric water cooler; Crossnore—furnishings for chapel.

☆ A rosette in the C.A.R. Society colors of red, white and blue was adopted. It was designed by Mr. John W. Finger of New York City, an Honorary President General of the SAR.

☆ On Washington's Birthday each year, a reception is held in Portland, Oregon, to welcome the newest naturalized citizens and the C.A.R. Societies are invited to assist with the reception.

☆ The Second Edition of the *C.A.R. Handbook* was printed.

☆ The Kathleen Douglass Memorial Collection of Dolls in Native Costumes was formally dedicated.

☆ After five years of employment, Miss Jean Jacobs left her position with C.A.R. in January 1956 to work for DAR. She remained with DAR from 1956 until her retirement in June 1995. She served many of those years in the office of the President General.

☆ Mrs. David D. Porter had been hired by C.A.R. as a part-time genealogist. Her organization and administrative skills were quickly recognized and she was given the position of Executive Secretary for C.A.R.

☆ The Sixty-first through the Sixty-third Annual Conventions were held in the Ballroom of the Mayflower Hotel in Washington, D.C.

☆ The SAR Traveling Banner went to Pennsylvania and the DAR Traveling Banner to New York.

☆ While at Mt. Vernon for the installation exercises, the members toured the Mansion after which, a box luncheon was enjoyed at the picnic grounds.

☆ The incoming Junior National President, Robert Carroll Barr, was elected and installed.

Junior National President
1956 – 1957

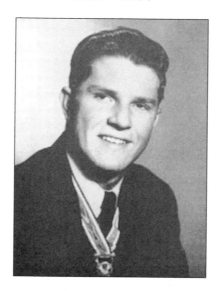

Robert Carroll Barr
Houston, Texas

☆ The theme for the year will be "SERVICE"—Service to God, our Country, our Homes, and Fellowman.

☆ The National Project is the restoration of "The Chapel of the Cross," a little chapel located at Mansdale, seventeen miles from Jackson, Mississippi.

☆ Support for the schools continued: Tamassee—an electric drinking fountain; Kate Duncan Smith—a planter for the farm; St. Mary's—type-writers; and Bacone College—desk lamps.

☆ In July 1956 the N.S.S.A.R. Society in France assumed the sponsorship of a new C.A.R. Society in Paris.

☆ The National President, Mrs. E. Stewart James and Mr. James offered two prizes to the two winners, a boy and a girl, who get the most new BOY members from July 1, 1956 to February 1957 Board Meeting. It was their belief that the C.A.R. was top-heavy with girls and they wished to equalize the membership by having this contest.

The winners received a week's vacation at "Church Hill Plantation," in Gloucester, Virginia, the home of the National President and her husband. The visit included trips to Williamsburg, Yorktown, and the Jamestown Festival.

☆ The first Regional Meeting of the North Central States was held in August.

☆ The SAR Traveling Banner went to New York and Washington and the DAR Traveling Banner went to New York.

☆ Mrs. Dwight D. Eisenhower, wife of the President, received the members at the White House.

☆ The incoming Junior National President, Dorothy Jacquelin Buckton, was elected and installed.

Junior National President
1957 – 1958

Dorothy Jacquelin Buckton
New York, New York

☆ The National Project: St. Mary's Indian School for Girls—General equipment including tents and camping equipment, phonographs, record, radios, money for library, and arts and crafts materials.

☆ A project started in 1957 by the Los Angeles Chapter, DAR, called Kenmore Youth Project, sends an outstanding state officer of the C.A.R. who resides in the southern section of California to the National Convention.

☆ The first Regional Meeting of the Mid-Atlantic States was held in July in Arlington, Virginia.

☆ Before the opening of the Annual Convention, the DAR had its Continental Congress and adopted the following resolution:

"Children of the American Revolution

Whereas, An urgent need for adequate, competent leadership to provide patriotic training for our own sons and daughters is recognized to exist; and

Whereas, That duty and responsibility rests squarely on the shoulders of our individual members and is of prime concern to our Society as an organization;

Resolved, That members of the chapters of the National Society, Daughters of the American Revolution be urged to provide proper senior leadership for societies of the Children of the American Revolution; and/or to give support by financial contributions as interested promoters or sponsors."

☆ On April 18, 1958, the Senior National Board adopted a resolution: On Establishment and Operation of THE NATIONAL ENDOWMENT FUND of the Children of the American Revolution.

☆ At the April National Board there was a bylaw change to drop the title "Junior" and use "National President" for members and add "Senior" to the present title for National President.

☆ During hurricane Hazel in 1954, the original C.A.R. Tree was severely damaged and taken down in 1958. The current C.A.R. Tree was planted near the Tomb of George and Martha Washington at Mt. Vernon on April 20, 1958, by Dorothy Buckton.

☆ The incoming National President, David Harley Kemker, Jr., and Senior National President, Mrs. John Whelchel Finger, were elected and installed.

1958–1960

National President 1958 – 1959	Senior National President 1958 – 1960

David Harley Kemker, Jr.
New Orleans, Louisiana

Mrs. John Whelchel Finger
New York, New York

☆ National Theme: "LEADERSHIP"

☆ National Project: St. Mary's School for Indian Girls—Kitchen equipment to be purchased and other items be listed for local Society projects for approximately $2,700.00.

☆ On May 29, a delegation of twenty-five N.S.C.A.R. members were ushered into the rotunda of the Capitol where the National President and Senior National President placed Wreaths of red and white flowers at the foot of each catafalque—one to the Unknown Soldier of the Korean conflict and the other to the Unknown Soldier of World War II.

☆ The first Regional Meeting of the Northwestern States was held in August.

☆ The first contribution to the C.A.R. National Endowment Fund was given, on October 15, 1958, by Mr. William M. Parker, Senior Honorary National Vice President, in honor of his wife.

☆ The Library-Museum transferred to Gadsby's Tavern a lady's sidesaddle from the old Lincoln estate in Harrisonburg, Virginia, for the front entry-office and a trundle-bed in the Pouch Room, as indefinite loans.

☆ A new committee was named American Literature at the suggestion of the National President.

☆ The members of the C.A.R. National Board were invited by the President General, SAR, Mr. Walter A. Wentworth, to hold their Annual National Board Meeting at the new National Headquarters on April 24, 1959. The Annual Board Meeting was held at the Headquarters on Massachusetts Avenue in Washington, D.C.

☆ The Sixty-fourth Annual Convention was held in the Ballroom of the Mayflower Hotel, Washington, D.C.

☆ The N.S.C.A.R. presented J. Edgar Hoover, Director of the Federal Bureau of Investigation, a citation as "Today's Patriot".

☆ The first C.A.R. Band was started by Mr. Wilbur D. Lockwood, Jr., who served as Senior Director.

☆ The DAR Traveling Banner went to Illinois and New York.

☆ The Society of the Cincinnati had a ceremony honoring the late Mrs. Larz Anderson, Past National Vice President, C.A.R., at the Anderson House in Washington, D.C.

☆ There was a special presentation of Smokey Bear, through the courtesy of The State Foresters' Association and the U. S. Forest Service.

☆ Alaska became a State Society and presented the state flag.

☆ The Memorial Service was held at the Washington National Cathedral.

☆ A tree planting ceremony at Old Presbyterian Meeting House, Alexandria, Virginia, near the Tomb of the Unknown Soldier of the American Revolution, honored Mrs. E. Stewart James, Honorary Senior National President.

☆ The incoming National President, Linda Tompkins Lange, was elected and installed.

Kay Krueger, Indiana State Chairman, Tomb of the Unknown Revolutionary Soldier Committee, and a friend shown with "Little Smokey" at his first public appearance in April 1959.

National President
1959 – 1960

Linda Tompkins Lange
Short Hills, New Jersey

☆ National Theme: ACTION

☆ The Connecticut Society, C.A.R., honored two freshmen cadets at the University of Connecticut who had achieved first honors in Marksmanship with trophies and twenty-five dollar United States Savings Bonds.

☆ The division of states divided the responsibility for the four issues of the *Children of the American Revolution Magazine*. This was to have each state concentrate on a specific issue.

☆ In June, 1959, the first Regional Meeting of the New England States was held.

☆ The Code of Ethics for C.A.R. National Elections was adopted October 6, 1959.

☆ This was the year that the C.A.R. sponsored Yorktown Day.

Beginning in 1959 Patriotic Education Week was changed from Columbus Day to Yorktown Day. Local Societies arrange for displays in libraries and stores, for governors and mayors to issue proclamations, and space in newspapers to name a few activities. For its hard work for patriotism the C.A.R. earned for the National Society a George Washington Honor Medal from Freedoms Foundation at Valley Forge. Much was done at Headquarters such as printing brochures, posters, stickers, participation ribbons and mailing the packets.

☆ Mrs. Richard M. Nixon, wife of the Vice President, visited C.A.R. National Headquarters.

☆ C.A.R. received the Freedoms Foundation award for Americana General Category. The Motion Picture Committee presented an award to John Wayne, Producer and star of *The Alamo*. The Radio and Television Committee presented a special award to Leslie Nielsen for his part in *The Swamp Fox*, a Walt Disney Production.

☆ On February 22, 1960, the California State Societies of DAR, C.A.R., SAR, and S.R. sponsored the dedication of the Court of Freedom of Forest Lawn Memorial Park in Glendale.

☆ The Sixty-fifth Annual Convention's Opening Night was in DAR Constitution Hall for the first time. The business sessions were in the Ballroom at the Mayflower Hotel in Washington, D.C.

☆ The SAR Traveling Banner went to Pennsylvania and the DAR to New York and Virginia. The Hawaii flag was presented.

☆ The incoming National President, Thomas Edward Senf, and Senior National President, Mrs. James Henry Summerville, were elected and installed.

George Washington Honor Medal from Freedoms Foundation at Valley Forge, Pennsylvania

110

1960–1962

| National President 1960 – 1961 | Senior National President 1960 – 1962 |

Thomas Edward Serf
New Britain, Connecticut

Mrs. James Henry Summerville
Charlotte, North Carolina

☆ National Theme: INTEREST

☆ National Projects: Air-condition C.A.R. National Headquarters; American Indians: Bacone Indian College—Library books and furnishing a dormitory room; St. Mary's School for Indian Girls—Laboratory equipment, movie projector and building fund.

☆ The Alaska SAR, DAR and C.A.R. saw the fulfillment of their joint project for the Alaska Methodist University in Anchorage on October 13, 1960. The plaque reads:

"OLD GLORY"
May her inspiration forever influence those
teaching and learning under her protection.
Privileged and Honored, we present
to

Margaret Mulford Lothrop (C.A.R. Member #1) with her mother's portrait (Harriett Mulford Stone Lothrop, Founder N.S.C.A.R.) at C.A.R National Headquarters during Annual Convention 1960

Alaska Methodist University
at Anchorage
its first campus flag and flagpole
October 13, 1960

**Alaska Society, Sons of the American Revolution
Col. John Mitchell Chapter, Daughters of the American Revolution
Denali Society, Children of the American Revolution**

☆ Mrs. William H. Pouch, National President 1937-1939, passed away on November 26, 1960.

☆ In March of 1961, the Texas Society marked the Old French Colony Cemetery in Dallas, the final resting place of many of those brave French colonists who came to Texas in 1855 to establish the Utopian colony of La Reunion. It also placed a marker on the Site of Confederate Fort 0.15 miles north which was surveyed in 1864 by Lt. Col. Albert M. Lea and built to fortify Gonzales against attacks by Federal Gunboats. It was constructed from stones of the Male Building of Gonzales College.

☆ On March 25, the first Regional Meeting of the Western States was held at Reno, Nevada.

☆ The SAR Traveling Banner went to Pennsylvania and the DAR Traveling Banner went to Texas.

☆ The National Society received a second George Washington Honor Medal from Freedoms Foundation at Valley Forge.

☆ The Statement of Policy for the Operation of Regions and Regional Meetings was revised on April 20, 1961.

☆ The incoming National President, Elizabeth Prince Bennett, was elected and installed.

National President
1961 – 1962

Elizabeth Prince Bennett
Washington, D.C.

☆ National Theme: A Goal; June-Purpose; September-Aim; December-Strive; March-Success.

☆ National Projects to the schools, Crossnore—black-top play area; Tamassee—canteen; Kate Duncan Smith—Library books.

☆ On June 17, 1961, the Massachusetts C.A.R. Society placed a wreath at the statue of Colonel William Prescott to commemorate the Battle of

Bunker Hill in 1775 at the base of Bunker Hill Monument in Charlestown, Massachusetts.

☆ On July 8, 1961, the Massachusetts C.A.R. held a service at the Cathedral of the Pines in Rindge, New Hampshire. The altar is dedicated to the Glory of God in memory of the American War Dead. The N.S.C.A.R. insignia was presented to Mr. Douglas Sloane, Founder of the Cathedral of the Pines, in memory of Mrs. Daniel M. Lothrop.

☆ Mrs. John P. Mosher (Ethel Vance), author of *The C.A.R. Creed*, died on July 26, 1961.

☆ On October 24, 1961, the N.S.C.A.R. dedicated part of the new playground equipment at Kate Duncan Smith DAR School.

☆ In November, the first Southwestern Regional Meeting was held in Denver, Colorado. The Colorado C.A.R. had a booth at Health Fair with an exhibit entitled *Our American Heritage*.

☆ On January 13, 1962, Dr. Mary T. Martin, co-founder of Crossnore School, passed away.

☆ The New York State C.A.R. presented a special citation to the New York Journal American for its outstanding work in conservation and for the film strip entitled: *Conservation and National Policy*.

☆ The Sixty-sixth Annual Convention was held for the first time at the Sheraton Park Hotel in Washington, D.C.

☆ The National President's Award was presented to Mr. Clark Kinnaird for his outstanding contribution to American Youth. He is the author of *Your America*, a King Features Syndicate.

☆ The SAR Traveling Banner went to New York and the DAR Traveling Banner went to Pennsylvania and Illinois.

☆ For the third year in a row the George Washington Honor Medal by Freedoms Foundation at Valley Forge was given to the N.S.C.A.R. for its sponsorship of Patriotic Education Week.

☆ The incoming National President, James A. Adkinson, Jr., and Senior National President, Mrs. W. Earle Hawley, were elected and installed.

1962–1964

National President	Senior National President
1962 – 1963	1962 – 1964

James A. Adkinson, Jr.	**Mrs. W. Earle Hawley**
Orlando, Florida	*Stratford, Connecticut*

☆ National Theme: AWARENESS—Past, Present, and Future.

☆ National Project: Patriotic Education Week with emphasis on SAR Poster Campaign "Keep U.S.A. First" with money allocated to St. Mary's School for Indian Girls.

☆ On May 26, 1962 the Pennsylvania State Society, C.A.R. was honored to be the first state society to present a program for the National Congress of the Sons of the American Revolution in Philadelphia.

☆ In June, The Major General James E. Fechet Award, sponsored by the N.S.C.A.R., was presented to the outstanding graduating cadet in speech competition at the Air Force Academy, Colorado Springs, Colorado. Major General Fechet was Chief of the Army Air Corps, 1927-1931, and was instrumental in the establishment of Randolph Field, "The West Point of the Air."

☆ In July, a $50.00 Savings Bond, for excellence in history and linguistic studies, was presented by the N.S.C.A.R. to a cadet at the United States Merchant Marine Academy at Kings Point, New York.

☆ On July 4, for the first time the District of Columbia Society of the Children of the American Revolution honored the memory of John W. Hunter who served in the Revolutionary War at the age of thirteen. He is buried in Congressional Cemetery, Washington, D.C.

☆ The Code of Ethics for C.A.R. National Elections was revised October 16, 1962, and the Standing Rules for C.A.R. Senior National Board of Management Meetings were adopted on February 4, 1963.

☆ On March 1, 1963, the first Endowment Fund Pin was received by Mrs. Frederic M. Senf of Connecticut.

☆ The Sixty-seventh Annual Convention was held at the Sheraton Park Hotel, Washington, D.C. California, Tennessee and Washington presented new state flags.

☆ The DAR Traveling Banner went to Pennsylvania and Virginia, and the SAR Traveling Banner went to Pennsylvania and Texas.

☆ Theodore C. Fearnow and Patrick Sheehan from the Forestry Service were presented with a check to cover the costs of constructing our National Trail in the Elizabeth Furnace Area of the George Washington National Park, near Harrisonburg, Virginia. This was the special conservation project for the year.

☆ The George Washington Honor Medal by Freedoms Foundation at Valley Forge was given to N.S.C.A.R. for the Americanism of its entry, the *Children of the American Revolution Magazine*, and its Patriotic Education Observance Week exhibit.

☆ The memorial service was held at the Washington National Cathedral.

☆ The incoming National President, Mary Huston Armstrong, was elected and installed.

National President
1963 – 1964

Mary Huston Armstrong
Columbia, Tennessee

☆ National Theme: REDEDICATION TO GOD AND COUNTRY

☆ National Project: Kate Duncan Smith DAR School and Tamassee DAR School—50/50 division.

☆ Life Promoter #1 was Mrs. Robert V. H. Duncan of Virginia.

☆ On August 3-9, 1963, there was a C.A.R. Mountain School Tour visiting Tamassee and Kate Duncan Smith DAR Schools.

☆ Honorary National President James A. Adkinson, Jr. presented a book to the museum entitled *Facts I Ought to Know About the Government of My Country* which was given to him at the Florida Conference. Inscribed on the flyleaf, in the handwriting of our founder Mrs. Daniel Lothrop, are the words "Presented to the Old North Bridge Society of Concord, Massachusetts by Mrs. Daniel Lothrop, 1897."

☆ The 1964 Annual Convention was held at the Sheraton Park Hotel in Washington, D.C.

☆ During the opening session of the 68th Annual Convention, the National President's Award was presented to the National Geographic Society for its outstanding contributions to American Youth. The Award was accepted by Dr. Melvin M. Payne, Executive Vice President.

☆ The George Washington Honor Medal from Freedoms Foundation was given for work in promoting patriotism among young people. Mr. Henry Francis, in presenting the award, said it was the first time he had ever presented one to a group which had won it for six consecutive years.

☆ The New Mexico state flag was presented.

☆ The memorial service was held at the Washington National Cathedral and the installation at Mount Vernon.

☆ The incoming National President, Van Rensselaer H. Sternbergh, and Senior National President, Mrs. Nile E. Faust were elected and installed.

1964–1966

National President 1964 – 1965	Senior National President 1964 – 1966

Van Rensselaer H. Sternbergh
Washington, D.C.

Mrs. Nile E. Faust
Concord, New Hampshire

☆ National Theme: FREEDOM'S CHALLENGE

☆ National Project: The National Endowment Fund. The Senior National President suggested that "money corsages" and "money centerpieces" be used at all State Conferences, Regional and Local Society Meetings and the money contributed to the Endowment Fund.

☆ On May 3, a marker was placed at the grave of James Foster, a Revolutionary soldier, buried at "Foster Mound" Cemetery on the plantation of James Foster near Natchez, Mississippi, by the Nathaniel Jeffries Society, C.A.R., Port Gibson, Mississippi.

☆ Mrs. Reuben Edward Knight, National President from 1945 to 1947, passed away on June 6, 1964.

☆ The Letitia Coxe Shelby DAR Chapter in California included the C.A.R. in its American Heritage activities, believing that it is part of the rightful heritage of our young people. On the sesquicentennial of the Star Spangled Banner, the DAR and C.A.R. members worked together to prepare a diorama of Mary Pickersgill and her daughter making the Flag that flew over Fort McHenry.

☆ The Pilot Rock DAR Chapter in Iowa used a special ceremony to welcome C.A.R. transfers to chapter membership and gave transfer honor awards to those who were outstanding.

☆ From 1965 to 1980 the Annual Conventions were held at the Sheraton Park Hotel in Washington, D.C.

☆ C.A.R. was the recipient of the George Washington Honor Medal of Freedoms Foundation for work in the field of Patriotic Freedom.

☆ The National President's Award, given by Mrs. John W. Finger, Honorary Senior National President, was presented to the American National Red Cross for its outstanding contributions to American Youth. It was accepted by General James F. Collins, President.

☆ The presiding officer read the following excerpts from a tribute to the C.A.R. from the Congressional Record of April 14.

"To encourage others in their youth work, the C.A.R presents a President's Award each year. This year Standard Oil of California will receive the awards for its Standard School Broadcast, the oldest program of fine music sponsored without commercial reference and widely used for classroom instruction.

"I feel that at this time when we hear so much adverse criticism of our young people that it is well to be remembered that there are many dedicated patriotic young people among us on whom we can depend to uphold the American way of life."

The remarks had been made by Representative W. J. B. Dorn of South Carolina on Thomas Jefferson's Birthday (April 13). This was the first time C.A.R. had been so honored.

☆ Alabama, Illinois and Ohio presented new state flags.

☆ The DAR Traveling Banner went to New York and the SAR Traveling Banner went to New Jersey.

☆ A special visit to the White House was arranged through the courtesy of the First Lady, Mrs. Lyndon B. Johnson.

☆ The incoming National President, Susan Hollingsworth Lewis, was elected and the installation ceremony was held in the hotel due to the weather.

National President
1965 – 1966

Susan Hollingsworth Lewis
Lafayette, Louisiana

☆ National Project: Increase Endowment Fund and get 3500 new members.

☆ Mrs. William Henry Sullivan, President General, NSDAR, announced that one item on the new DAR Honor Roll asks if the DAR Chapters "provide Senior Leadership for C.A.R."

☆ On May 23, 1965, the Washington-Lee Society, C.A.R., in Arlington, Virginia, placed a marker at the site of Matildaville chartered in 1790 by Light Horse Harry Lee and Associates.

☆ On July 4, David Lee Cherney, National First Vice President, C.A.R., had the privilege to lay the National Society's wreath at the grave of General Lafayette in the Cimetiere de Picpus, Paris, France.

☆ The Pig Iron Trail at Elizabeth Furnace, an historical nature trail built in cooperation with the Forest Service of the United States Department of

Agriculture, using nation-wide donations from members of C.A.R., was dedicated on October 16, 1965. Credit for the project goes back to James A. Adkinson, Jr., National President, and Mrs. W. Earle Hawley, Senior National President. The ceremony took place in an outdoor theater in the George Washington National Forest near Harrisonburg, Virginia.

☆ Mrs. James H. Summerville, Senior National President from 1960 to 1962, passed away on February 5, 1966.

☆ The District of Columbia Society raised money to purchase a German Shepherd Dog for K-9 duty which was given to the Metropolitan Police Department and was named CAR.

☆ At the Coffee Hour held in the C.A.R. Museum preceding the Annual Convention, the guests were delighted to see the completed first section of the C.A.R. MUSEUM RENOVATION.

☆ State flags from South Dakota and Wisconsin were presented.

C.A.R. Museum Renovation—First section

☆ The DAR Traveling Banner went to New York and the SAR Traveling Banner to Virginia.

☆ For the seventh consecutive year the George Washington Honor Medal by Freedoms Foundation at Valley Forge was given to the N.S.C.A.R.

☆ The incoming National President, David Lee Cherney, and Senior National President, Mrs. Edwin H. Tiemeyer, were elected and installed.

1966–1968

National President 1966 – 1967	Senior National President 1966 – 1968

David Lee Cherney
Redwood City, California

Mrs. Edwin H. Tiemeyer
Cincinnati, Ohio

☆ National Theme: THIS IS MY COUNTRY

☆ National Project: Improvement and modernization of the display facilities in the C.A.R. Museum.

☆ On June 6, 1966, the New Mexico C.A.R. and DAR, in cooperation with the United States Forest Service, placed an historic-conservation marker at Whitewater Canyon, Gila National Forest where rich gold and silver deposits were discovered about 1889.

☆ The California State Society restored a typical schoolroom of the 1890 era located in the Railroad Transportation Museum, Dunsmuir, California.

☆ Mrs. E. Stewart James, National President from 1955 to 1958, passed away on August 3, 1966.

✭ On October 15, 1966, officers and members of the Pennsylvania State Society, C.A.R., met with representatives of the Pennsylvania Forestry Association and the Bowman's Hill Wildflower Preserve Committee in Washington Crossing State Park. The park encompasses the area occupied by the Continental Army prior to the crossing of the Delaware to attack Trent's Town on Christmas Eve, 1776. The conservation project was the landscaping of the entrance which included the state tree and flower, Hemlock and Mountain Laurel. A bronze plaque, set in a boulder at the site, marks the State Society's participation.

✭ The Castle Thunder C.A.R. Society of Catonsville, Maryland, presented two texturized American Flags to the Maryland School for the Blind and to the Rolling Road School for the handicapped.

✭ On October 24, 1966, Mrs. Emily Noyes Davis passed away. She was the First President of the First C.A.R. Society, Old North Bridge Society, Concord, Massachusetts, appointed by Mrs. Lothrop in 1895.

✭ The Connecticut Society, C.A.R., donated a check to the Noah Webster House Foundation, Inc., to help in its restoration.

✭ On December 11, at the Junction of Highways 133 and 134 in Oak Ridge, Louisiana, the Prairie Jefferson Society, C.A.R., held a service to mark Prairie Jefferson, now called Oak Ridge, and to commemorate Mrs. Lillian Pipes Barham, Organizing President of Prairie Jefferson Society, C.A.R. The marker, donated by the Abram Morehouse DAR Chapter, reads:

> "Erected by Abram Morehouse Chapter, D.A.R., to mark the site of Prairie Jefferson and to commemorate Lillian Pipes Barham, Organizing Senior President of the C.A.R. Society which bears the name of the early settlement founded by Abram Morehouse in 1807 on part of the original Spanish Grant to Baron de Bastrop in 1797."

✭ To benefit the C.A.R. Museum, a plaque and Red Apple Pin were approved to be presented to each donor of $1,000. On February 9, 1967, the first donation of $1,000 honored Paul M. Niebell, Jr., President, 1966-1967, of Harriett M. Lothrop Society, D.C.C.A.R. The second one went to Miss Katharine Matthies of Connecticut, and the third to Mr. and Mrs. Walter English of Ohio.

Dale Louis Harris, D.C.C.A.R. member, wrote a letter to Mrs. Meriwether Post, heiress to the Post Cereal Company, telling her about the N.S.C.A.R. Museum and asking her for a donation of $1,000 to become a Major Benefactor. To his great surprise she sent a check.

✭ For the 8th time, the N.S.C.A.R. received the Freedoms Foundation award for outstanding achievement in bringing about a better understanding of the American way of life—American Heritage Theme.

☆ Tamassee DAR School is most grateful for what the N.S.C.A.R. has given it. One of the most popular places on campus is the Student Center, a gift of the National Society. The boys and girls get together there after classes for cokes, snacks and fellowship. Another gift is the beauty shop for girls and the barber shop for boys.

☆ At the Convention Banquet on April 22, 1967, David Lee Cherney, National President, called Mr. James Johnson to the platform, saying:

> "I want to thank Mrs. Sullivan for appointing Mr. Jim Johnson for being the DAR watchdog for the C.A.R. Museum Renovation; because, after his official work was done—the approval of our plans—he became a most determined volunteer and was a key person in the advising, planning, and construction of the beginning of our Museum Renovation."

> * * * * *

> "Mr. Johnson, I'm happy to tell you that, by official action of the National Society, the 1966-67 National Project monies for the C.A.R. Museum Renovation have been designated in your honor so that your name may be placed on the permanent Plaque of Major Benefactors of the C.A.R. Museum."

☆ The 1967 National President's Award, given by Mrs. John W. Finger, was presented to the United States Department of Agriculture for 100 years of outstanding service to the youth of rural America. It was accepted by Mr. John A. Baker, Assistant Secretary of Agriculture.

☆ Colorado, Florida, Kentucky and Maryland presented new state flags.

☆ The DAR Traveling Banner went to New York and the SAR Traveling Banner went to Virginia.

☆ Two students from St. Mary's School for Indian Girls dressed in tribal costume and representatives from Crossnore and Kate Duncan Smith DAR Schools were present at the Convention.

☆ The incoming National President, Jane Wells Freeny, was elected and installed.

National President
1967 – 1968

Jane Wells Freeny
Baltimore, Maryland

☆ National Theme: MEMBERSHIP, MUSEUM, AND MAGAZINE.

☆ National Project: Renovation of C.A.R. Museum.

☆ The foyer outside the new Senior National President's Office was furnished with a new console with a Delft brick flower holder with an Eighteenth Century bouquet on top and above a beautiful Chippendale mirror. The money for these purchases came from the Elise H. Parcells Fund of the General Lord Stirling Society, Brooklyn, New York, which was organized February 22, 1924, and from members of the Women of '76 Chapter, DAR, Brooklyn, New York.

☆ The Virginia Society, C.A.R. placed a bronze C.A.R. marker at the grave of Mrs. E. Stewart James in Ware Episcopal Church Cemetery, Gloucester, Virginia. The ceremony honoring the late Mrs. James for her C.A.R. accomplishments, took place at 1:00 PM on Saturday, the 26th of August, a year and a day after her funeral service.

A new Hammond organ with chimes was dedicated on Sunday, September 10, 1967, at St. Mary's School for Indian Girls, Springfield, South Dakota. The organ was a bequest of Mrs. E. Stewart James. A brass plate reads as follows:

"In memory of Mr. Ellerson Stewart James, Honorary Senior National Vice President, Children of the American Revolution, and Mrs. Ellerson Stewart James, Honorary Senior National President, Children of the American Revolution."

☆ A gavel of Washington Elm was presented to Sally Glacken Society at its organizing ceremony, held Constitution Day, September 17, 1967, at the Earl C. Douglas home in Seattle, Washington. The gavel was made by students of the woodwork shop of Garfield High School. It is made of wood from the historic tree which grew on the University of Washington campus. Mr. Joe Marshall, Counselor, who made the presentation, told how the tree grew from a cutting of the Washington Elm, under which General George Washington took command of the Continental Forces during the American Revolution.

☆ Mildred Furr Black, Assistant Executive Secretary of the N.S.C.A.R. for seven years, passed away on September 26, 1967. In her memory, a tea pot with stand, New Hall English porcelain, circa 1795, was added to the C.A.R. Museum collection.

☆ The C.A.R. National Headquarters converted its present filing system to an IBM automated system which took approximately six months.

☆ The Connecticut Society, C.A.R., held its Forty-second Annual State Conference in Slater Memorial Hall of the Norwich Free Academy on March 23, 1968. In summing up the year's activities, Jonathan E. Potter, President, told of the C.A.R. project of financially helping some of the historic homes in Connecticut. The recipients were the Ellsworth Homestead in Windsor, the Jonathan Trumbull House in Lebanon, the Eells Stowe House in Milford, and the Amos Morris House in New Haven.

☆ For the ninth consecutive year, the C.A.R. was presented with the Freedoms Foundation Award by Mr. Milton E. Canter, Trustee of Freedoms Foundation at Valley Forge, for our excellent work in Patriotic Education.

☆ The Arkansas State Conservation project was a Willow Oak tree planted at MacArthur Park in Little Rock. It was paid for jointly by the Arkansas State Society and the Texarkana Society. A plaque was provided by the City of Little Rock.

☆ The DAR and S.A.R. Traveling Banners were presented to New York, Pennsylvania and New Jersey respectively.

☆ Four new state flags were given to the National Society by Arkansas, Nevada, Oklahoma and South Carolina.

☆ The incoming National President, Thomas Walter Scott, and Senior National President, Mrs. Byron W. Vanderbilt, were elected and installed.

1968–1970

National President 1968 – 1969	Senior National President 1968 – 1970

Thomas Walter Scott
Arlington, Virginia

Mrs. Byron M. Vanderbilt
Scotch Plains, New Jersey

☆ National Project: Historic marker at U. S. Hill Observation Point, El Camino Real, Carson National Forest, New Mexico.
☆ Society Activities:

The Pathfinder DAR Chapter, Port Gibson, Mississippi, and Captain Thomas White Society, C.A.R. of Yazoo City, Mississippi, cooperated to erect and dedicate a bronze marker honoring a Revolutionary War Soldier, Captain Thomas White, Jr., buried in Claiborne County, Mississippi, three miles south of Port Gibson on the Natchez Trace. The marker was dedicated at Wintergreen Cemetery in an impressive ceremony.

The New Mexico State Society, C.A.R., dedicated a marker on July 7, 1968, at Cloudcroft for "Pennies for Pines" Reforestation Project presented by Yucca Society, Jorando del Muerto Society, and Richard Merrell Society.

The Red Cedar River Society in Cedar Falls, Iowa, dedicated an historical marker on July 16, 1968, in memory of Thunderwoman, a Winnebago Indian, buried in the family cemetery of James Newell, first white settler in Washington township.

☆ Yorktown Day of 1968 was hosted by the National Society of the Children of the American Revolution since it was the responsibility of C.A.R. to lead the day's activities.

☆ Each year at Christmas time, the Old Stage Road Society, C.A.R., Brunswick, Tennessee, celebrates the "Hanging of the Greens." With the Brunswick Road Garden Club; the Shelby Chapter, SAR; and the Zachariah Davies Chapter, DAR; the young people decorate both sides of a gigantic highway overpass on Interstate 40 at Brunswick, less than ten miles from Memphis.

☆ State Activities:

At the Virginia State Conference in February 1969 a C.A.R. Citation was presented to the Rockefeller Foundation and Colonial Williamsburg, Inc. for their roles in fostering interest in the heritage of our country.

The Ohio State Project was the purchase of a silver tea pot, made in Sheffield, England, between 1830-40 by Philip Ashberry & Sons, and presented to the Orange Johnson House in Worthington.

C.A.R. members from Louisiana gathered in New Orleans in St. Louis Cemetery #2 at the grave of Major General Pierre Denis de la Ronde II for a marker dedication. General de la Ronde served as a cadet in the Galvez Expedition during the Revolution, and was promoted to lieutenant during this duty. He later served as a colonel under command of Andrew Jackson at the Battle of New Orleans, and as Commanding General of the Louisiana Militia.

On April 5, 1969, the Massachusetts State Conference announced the successful completion of the State Project—the raising of $100 for an Endowment Fund Pin. On Easter Sunday, the State President presented the pin to Miss Margaret Lothrop, C.A.R. Member #1.

☆ It was with pride and pleasure that C.A.R. received the following communication from Dr. Kenneth Wells, President, Freedoms Foundation at Valley Forge:

"It is my great privilege to convey to you the congratulations of the officers and trustees of Freedoms Foundation upon the selection, by the distinguished 1968 National Awards Jury, of the National Society, Children of the American Revolution as a principal awardee in the Americana General Category for its observance of Patriotic Education Week."

This award the 4-inch George Washington Honor Medal encased in a 7-inch square block of Lucite, was presented at the awards luncheon at Valley Forge on February 22nd. It was received by Tom Scott, National President, and Barrett Matthews, National Chairman, Patriotic Education.

☆ Dr. Kenneth D. Wells, President of Freedoms Foundation, accepted the "President's Award" given by our society in acknowledgment of Freedoms Foundation's outstanding patriotic work.

☆ The DAR Traveling Banner went to Pennsylvania and the SAR Traveling Banner to Virginia.

☆ Mr. Burton M. Langhenry, representing Freedoms Foundation at Valley Forge, presented Thomas Walter Scott, National President, a Principal Award, the Encased George Washington Honor Medal, for the work done by the National Society during Patriotic Education Week. Mrs. Byron M. Vanderbilt, Senior National President, was privileged to hold the Distinguished Service Award which is presented to awardees who have received ten George Washington Honor Medal Awards.

☆ The incoming National President, Sharon Kay Krueger, was elected and installed.

National President
1969 – 1970

Sharon Kay Krueger
South Bend, Indiana

☆ National Theme: RESOLVE, PLAN, AND PERFORM.

☆ National Project: In cooperation with the National Park Service—provide wallpaper for "The Wayside," Concord, Massachusetts.

☆ On June 21, 1969, a Memorial Wreath was placed at the grave of Mrs. Harriett M. Lothrop, founder of N.S.C.A.R., by Mrs. Byron M. Vanderbilt, Senior National President, and Sharon Kay Krueger, National President, at Authors' Ridge, Sleepy Hollow Cemetery, Concord, Massachusetts. The dedication prayer was given by Thomas McCune Slick, National Treasurer.

☆ July 9, 1969, was the day of the dedication of the National Project: El Camino Real. The portion of the Camino Real that is inside our present boundaries is the oldest and most historic road in the United States. For three and one-half centuries the Camino Real was the only north-south commerce route in the entire Southwest. It served as the only connection between New Mexico and New Spain. Preceding the unveiling of the historic trails marker, a group of conquistadores dressed in their colorful costumes, which included armor and plumes, saluted the C.A.R. and the U. S. Forest Service in Spanish and English.

★ On October 18, 1969, an historical marker placed by the Louisiana State Tourist Commission at Ashland Plantation, near New Orleans, was dedicated by the Louisiana State Society, C.A.R., in ceremonies climaxing the state's observance of Patriotic Education Week. C.A.R. members toured Ashland and visited two other River Road plantations: San Francisco and Houmas House.

★ For the first time, the Connecticut State Society, C.A.R., presented the Annual Church Service of the Hereditary Patriotic Societies, a traditional celebration of thanks held in cooperation with twenty-four other patriotic societies in Connecticut. The choir, entirely made up of C.A.R. members sang the Anthem, The Battle Hymn of the Republic, thus ending the Patriotic Education Week—1969.

75TH ANNIVERSARY

Our 75th Anniversary was celebrated starting with the Museum Renovation Dedication on February 1st, 1970. Pat Nicol, National Librarian-Curator wrote the following:

"From Rhode Island to Colorado and from Massachusetts to Florida, the more than 400 members and friends came to attend our Museum Renovation Dedication on the beautiful sunny day, February 1, 1970.

"C.A.R. members, as guides, explained our 56 cases of exhibits telling a story of the early history of our country based on the 'faith of our fathers'."

The President General, NSDAR, accepted a "surprise" plaque, made possible through the individual contributions of the Museum Renovation Committee, to the NSDAR " appreciation of the many things done for C.A.R. over the past 75 years and particularly for the moral support of this project."

In honor of our 75th Birthday, the Special Museum Event and lovely reception, hosted by the NSDAR at the same time, made it possible for all to enjoy the exhibits in the DAR Museum including a special display of items from the "Children's Attic."

Added attractions during the afternoon were Founder Mrs. Lothrop's green velvet dress, modeled by Miss Elizabeth Bennett, Senior National Treasurer, and the popular 18th century music tunes played on a six-stringed "laute" and sung by Taylor Vrooman, balladeer from Colonial Williamsburg.

Pictured at the unveiling of the plaque honoring Major Benefactors from left to right are: Miss Jane Wells Freeny, Honorary National President; Mrs. Byron M. Vanderbilt, Senior National President; Miss Sharon Kay Krueger National President; and Mr. Thomas W. Scott, Honorary National President

134

The March 1970 issue of the *Children of the American Revolution Magazine* had a picture of Harriett M. Lothrop on the cover honoring the Seventy-fifth Anniversary.

☆ The Annual Convention had a wonderful announcement. We're over the top: The year 1969-70 saw the original $100,000 goal of the National Endowment Fund reached and exceeded. To help the Endowment Fund grow, official 75th Anniversary Corsages were sold.

☆ New Hampshire and Oregon presented their state flags.

☆ The National Society was honored for the eleventh consecutive year by receiving the George Washington Honor Medal Award from Freedoms Foundation.

☆ The All States Chorus along with the National Board, gave an excellent selection of songs illustrating American life *Through 75 Years*. Among the songs were *In the Good Old Summertime*; *Keep the Home Fires Burning*, *It's a Grand Old Flag*, and *Yankee Doodle Dandy*.

☆ The Virginia State Society received both the DAR and SAR Traveling Banners.

☆ The National President's Award was presented to The Continental Insurance Companies for outstanding contribution to American Youth.

☆ As C.A.R. completes its Diamond Anniversary year, the DAR may well look with pride and affection as they again "behold an army" united in its effort to be good citizens in the world of the future while maintaining knowledge and respect for the tradition which made America great. Many of the things spoken of by Mrs. Lothrop have come to pass. Through the guidance of their parent organization, the young C.A.R. members are able to find a haven of stability in today's chaos as they prepare to take the places of the current leaders. Continued encouragement, help, and leadership from the DAR are a must, for it is through helping to train tomorrow's leaders that DAR will find today's greatest fulfillment.

As it moves into its fourth quarter of a century, true to its motto, "For God and Country," the C.A.R. truly stands as an army that shall never be conquered.

☆ The incoming National President, Lance David Ehmcke, and Senior National President, Mrs. Robert S. Hudgins, were elected and installed in the Sheraton Park Hotel due to the weather.

1970–1972

National President 1970 – 1971	Senior National President 1970 – 1972

Lance David Ehmcke *Cleghorn, Iowa*	**Mrs. Robert S. Hudgins** *Charlotte, North Carolina*

☆ National Theme: SPIRIT OF '76—TAKE PRIDE IN AMERICA

☆ National Project: Renovation of the C.A.R. Board Room in Memorial Continental Hall.

☆ On May 14, 1970, N.S.C.A.R. Member #1 passed away. The following appeared in the June 1970 issue of the Children of the American Revolution Magazine:

IN MEMORIAM
Miss Margaret Mulford Lothrop—C.A.R. Member #1
July 27, 1884—May 14, 1970

"Something wonderful is gone with the passing of Miss Lothrop. She was the daughter of our founder and throughout seventy-five eventful years was Member Number One of the National Society, Children of the American Revolution. She was the C.A.R. Senior National Vice President for life, a DAR member, a traveler, college professor, a Red Cross volunteer overseas during the First Great War, lecturer, historian, and an irreplaceable link with the rich past of her home The Wayside. There is one title of which she was more proud than any other. Miss Margaret was an American.

"Those who knew her, loved her. Those who met her, admired and respected her. To speak with Margaret Lothrop brought courage to the heart.

"Something wonderful is gone. And yet, the inspiration of a life of service based in deep Christian Faith and dedication to the American ideal remains for those of us whose duty it is to preserve the nation which she so loved."

☆ A familiar landmark in McLean, Virginia, Salona is noted as the only "Emergency White House" in American History. The home of Parson and Mrs. William Maffitt, it served as a refuge for the President of the United States and his wife, James and Dolley Madison, on August 24, 1814, when they were forced to flee from the White House. This event occurred when the British, in the War of 1812, invaded the city of Washington and burned many of the government buildings including the White House. Reputedly built about 1802, Salona has become known through the years as "the place of great hospitality." Restored to its former charm, Salona is now the home of Clive DuVal II, a delegate to Virginia's General Assembly. On May 15, 1970, members and guests of Freedom Hill Society, C.A.R., were entertained by Mrs. DuVal and Clive DuVal, III. In an appropriate ceremony, Salona was marked with a plaque by the society followed by a reception in the gardens of Salona.

☆ On Memorial Day, 1970, Yucca Society, Portales, New Mexico, participated in Community Memorial Day activities with Dwight Denton, laying the C.A.R. Wreath honoring Veterans of the Viet Nam War. As he laid the wreath Bobbi Jo Hawk read the poem titled *I Am An American*. Other Yucca members distributed programs and the Society President led the Pledge of Allegiance. This was one of our many combination Patriotic Education and Community Service projects during the year.

☆ Annually, the city of Philadelphia celebrates *Freedom Week* as a prelude to the 4th of July. On June 29, 1970, the Pennsylvania State Society participated in a flag raising ceremony and tribute to Revolutionary War dead in Washington Park behind Independence Hall. The C.A.R. distinguished itself by being the only organization to participate in the *Freedom Week* celebration. Thirteen C.A.R. members from various Pennsylvania Societies raised the commonwealth flags of the thirteen original colonies as Miss Liberty Belle, representing the city of Philadelphia, raised the Betsy Ross Flag. The flag raising was followed by a presentation by the Mount Vernon Guard, which was very befitting of the occasion.

☆ In a departure from the usual, young Marylanders played an important part in welcoming new citizens at the June 30, 1970, Naturalization Court in Rockville. Janis Hensley of Chevy Chase, State President of Maryland State Society, C.A.R., gave the welcoming address to new citizens. Two members of the Ark and Dove Society, Silver Spring, presented flags to each person taking the oath of allegiance.

☆ The Fourth Edition of the C.A.R. Handbook was published and the Code of Ethics for C.A.R. National Elections was amended.

☆ In March 1971, the Chief Catfish Society, C.A.R., presented the Pennsylvania State Project—the Bradford House in Washington, Pennsylvania.

☆ On April 17, 1971, The Wayside, home of the Concord Muster Master and later of three American Authors, Nathaniel Hawthorne, Louisa May Alcott, and Harriett M. Lothrop, was dedicated as a part of the Minute Man National Historical Park and opened to the public for touring. Lance Ehmcke remarked of our pride in being able to help with this renovation project. Purchasing period wallpaper for The Wayside was the 1969-70 C.A.R. National Project. In recognition of this assistance, the National Park Service presented C.A.R. with an engraved, silver "Revere" bowl. With the benediction and ribbon-cutting by dignitaries, the ceremony was over.

☆ The 76th Annual Convention took place on April 23, 1971, and a Keynote address by Brigadier General Daniel James, Jr., USAF, Deputy Assistant Secretary of Defense (Public Affairs), was the highlight of Friday Evening's session. Representatives from St. Mary's School for Indian Girls and Crossnore School brought greetings.

☆ Freedoms Foundation at Valley Forge presented the distinguished Service Plaque to the N.S.C.A.R. for its nationwide Patriotic Education Week activities under the *Take Pride in America* and *Government is People* programs.

☆ A new Georgia state flag was presented and Vermont was recognized as a newly reorganized State Society. The DAR Traveling Banner went to Tennessee and the SAR Traveling Banner went to Illinois. National dues were raised to $4.00.

This is an older part of the house where Mrs. Lothrop would sit, rock, and dream about new plots for the Five Little Pepper Series which she wrote under the pen name Margaret Sidney

☆ The National President's Award was presented to Walt Disney Productions for its outstanding entertaining and educational contributions to American youth.

☆ The incoming National President, Jane Elizabeth Hardy, was elected and installed.

National President
1971 – 1972

Jane-Elizabeth Hardy
Stratford, Connecticut

☆ National Theme: Government of the People—Strive to Keep it Great.

☆ National Project: Renovation of the C.A.R. National Board Room.

☆ Carlene and Bruce Hamilton are believed to be the first Navajo Indians to become members of C.A.R.

☆ The Senior National Board of Management voted to change the Bylaws to reduce the Regions from 10 to 9. The Advisory Board passed the following motion: "At the close of the current term of each Senior National Vice President of the Regions, the monies in the Regional Treasury shall be equally divided by the number of States who have appropriated their money to the Regional Treasury. The shares of those States changing Regions are to be forwarded immediately to the new Senior National Vice President of the new Region."

☆ During an impressive Dedication ceremony on Sunday, June 13, 1971, with Miss Georgia Bourne, State President of Indiana, C.A.R., presiding, Miss Heidi Eikenberry, Honorary State President, presented Indiana and the City of Indianapolis with an historic marker commemorating the proud past of Camp Sullivan, better known to Indianapolis residents as Military Park.

☆ On August 2, 1971, by plane, bus, train and car, C.A.R. members came to the Nation's Capital for a definite purpose: to learn of our Federal Government, of its problems, policies and operations. There were 61 members and Senior Leaders gathered for a week of "Government of the People." An old friend of C.A.R., Mr. Mal Hardy, Chief of Cooperative Forest Fire Prevention, brought the "good word" from Smokey Bear, and told of the plans for the Woodsy Owl campaign. Woodsy fought pollution on posters and billboards across the Nation during the year. Visits were made to the Forest Service, the Great Hall of the Department of Justice, the State Department and the Pentagon. They had a night tour of Washington and a boat trip to Mount Vernon. After a full week they departed for home to share their experiences within their communities, telling that this is a GOVERNMENT OF THE PEOPLE; a government concerned about its problems; a government working day by day to STRIVE TO KEEP IT GREAT. The National President, Jane-Elizabeth Hardy, made the trip possible.

☆ On Tamassee DAR School's program, recognition was given to the N.S.C.A.R. for the year's contributions as well as a Partial College Tuition for a boy.

☆ On April 20, 1972, the Resolution on The National Endowment Fund was amended.

☆ The *Children of the American Revolution Magazine* won the Freedoms Foundation at Valley Forge Distinguished Service Award for 1972, the George Washington Honor Medal. This is the first year the *Children of the American Revolution Magazine* has won a Freedoms Foundation Award; however, this is the 13th consecutive year that the N.S.C.A.R. has won a Freedoms Foundation award.

☆ The National President's Award was presented to Keep America Beautiful, Inc. of New York City.

☆ The incoming National President, Philip Field Horne, and Senior National President, Mrs. Roy D. Allan, were elected and installed.

1972–1974

National President	Senior National President
1972 – 1973	1972 – 1974

Philip Field Horne	**Mrs. Roy D. Allan**
Valhalla, New York	*Cincinnati, Ohio*

☆ National Theme: Know Your America—The Key to Your Future

☆ National Project: $1,000 Scholarship to a 1973 Graduate of Tamassee and $100 Scholarship for a Graduate of St. Mary's School for Indian Girls

☆ In a meeting of the N.S.C.A.R. Bicentennial of the United States of America Committee, prior to the June meeting of the Senior National Board of Management, a conservation project was decided upon entitled *Two Hundred Trees*. Each local society from coast to coast is urged to plant 200 trees for the 200 years of our country by 1976, the year of our nation's Bicentennial observance.

☆ On June 17, 1972, members attending the Pennsylvania State Conference, in Washington, Pennsylvania, toured the Meadowcroft Village, an early American restored village. Michael Mohr, State President, presented four items of pewter as his State Project. At the banquet, each guest received a pine seedling to be planted in keeping with our Conservation Bicentennial Project.

☆ *The Wayside* at Concord, Massachusetts, was the recipient of two photographs of our Founder, Mrs. Daniel Lothrop. Presentation of the photographs was made by Ruth Burns Ruggles, National Librarian-Curator, to the National Park Service, on June 21, 1972. The photographs were duplicates of pictures the National Society owns, and were helpful in identifying a hat of Mrs. Lothrop's which the Park Service wishes to display.

☆ The Pre-organization Meeting of the El Camino Real Society in Mexico City, Mexico, was held on July 10, 1972.

☆ The First Annual Great Lakes Regional Meeting was held July 28 in South Bend, Indiana. On August 11, 1972, it was the first year to welcome the States of Maryland and District of Columbia into the Eastern Region in Reading, Pennsylvania.

☆ At the request of the National Board, the Senior National Board of Management passed the following ruling on October 17, 1972: "That members of the National Board be made responsible for informing respective successors of the duties, responsibilities and problems of the office and suggestions and encouragement for carrying out the work of the office; this to be accomplished in person at the National Convention." On the same day, the Code of Ethics for C.A.R. National Elections was amended.

☆ On January 27, 1973, the Union Camp Corporation received its first public recognition for its gift of the 50,000 acre tract of the Great Dismal Swamp including Lake Drummond. The Virginia State Society presented an appropriately engraved plaque to a representative of the Corporation during the Annual State Conference in Richmond.

☆ The Statement of Policy for the Operation of Regions and Regional Meetings was revised on February 2, 1973.

☆ During the Ohio State Conference in Columbus on March 3 was the presentation of its $200.00 State Project check to the Zoo for the care and preservation of the American Eagle.

☆ On March 24, members attending the Michigan Society State Conference, in Marshall, were told of the state project which is the making of a nature trail for blind and visually handicapped . Construction is to start in the spring when a trail is cleared, perfectly flat, wider than the average, and a chain strung through wooden posts, complete with a braille legend of the surrounding area.

☆ The Annual Convention had several outstanding events:

An Ohio State Project was A Major Benefactor for the C.A.R. Museum.

A Freedoms Foundation Award recognized the *Children of the American Revolution Magazine*.

Indiana presented a new flag. The DAR Traveling Banner went to Illinois and the SAR Traveling Banner went to Pennsylvania.

The National Presidents' Award was presented to the Colonial Williamsburg Foundation.

☆ The Incoming National President, Margaret Ann Coffroth, was elected and installed.

National President
1973 – 1974

Margaret Ann Coffroth
Sacramento, California

☆ National Theme: Today's Work—Tomorrow's Future
☆ National Project: An endangered species project to be worked out by the two National Presidents with an agency of the Federal Government
☆ Upon the recommendation of the National Board, the Senior National Board of Management, at the June 1973 special meeting, changed the C.A.R. Creed to read:

I believe in the Children of the American Revolution as an organization for the training of young people in true patriotism and love of country, in order that they shall be better fitted for American Citizenship.

As a descendant of the Founders of my Country, I believe that my birthright brings a responsibility to carry on their work, and that as the boys and girls of 1776 took an active part in the War for Independence so the boys and girls of today have a definite work to do for their Country. As a member of the Children of the American Revolution, I believe it is my duty to use my influence to create a deeper love of country, a loyal respect for its Constitution and reverence for its Flag, among the young people with whom I come in contact.

☆ The Senior National Board of Management adopted the Guidelines for State Projects as follows:

1. The proposed State Project must be in keeping with the objectives and programs of the National Society, Children of the American Revolution.
2. The time element, for completion of the project, should be carefully considered. The Project should be completed within the term of the State President.
3. The proposal should be reasonable in scope and cost. It should not be so expensive as to preclude participation in approved National Projects.

☆   June 30, 1973

Mrs. Roy D. Allan
National Society Children of the
American Revolution
1776 D Street, Northwest
Washington, D.C. 20006

Dear Mrs. Allan:

I would like to express my appreciation for your efforts on my behalf.

I am very grateful that I was chosen to be the recipient of the $1,000.00 scholarship award of the National Society Children of the American Revolution presented to me at Tamassee-Salem High School graduation ceremonies on May 20, 1973.

This gift is certainly one of the main factors in helping to secure my first year at Clemson University where I have been accepted as a pre-architecture student.

Very truly yours,
Mark Williams
P .O. Box 307
South Miami, Florida 33143

☆ On July 19-20, the Great Plains Regional Meeting was held at St. Mary's School for Indian Girls and thanks went to Mr. and Mrs. Kenyon Cull for making it possible to meet there for the first time.

☆ In October, the Massachusetts State Society members, adults and some boys at Hillside School in Marlborough planted 2500 pine and spruce seedlings to be known as the C.A.R. Forest. This made Massachusetts one of the first states to complete the National Bicentennial Project.

☆ On October 15, the N.S.C.A.R. dedicated its newly-renovated C.A.R. Board Room, styled after a Colonial Meeting Room. This was the 1970-1972 National Project during the terms of National Presidents Lance D. Ehmcke and Jane-Elizabeth Hardy, and Mrs. Robert S. Hudgins, Senior National President.

☆ The N.S.C.A.R. announced that the December 1973 issue of the *Children of the American Revolution Magazine* would be the last in the present format. The March 1974 issue . . . At the Crossroads would be four pages. Since the costs of paper and printing had risen sharply in recent months, there was no way we could continue our sixty-four page magazine and were forced to "cut back."

☆ Bicentennial Projects:

Florida State Society placed a Highway marker for the Battle of Thomas Creek.

Illinois State Society planted an herb garden at the Patton Pioneer cabin at Lexington.

Texas State Society planted 3,000 pine and oak trees.

Wisconsin State Society planted 400 trees at "Surgeons Quarters" historic site.

☆ At the Annual Convention the National Society received the Freedoms Foundation Distinguished Service Award for work in Patriotic Education.

☆ The National Presidents' Award was presented to General Motors Corporation.

☆ The DAR Traveling Banner was presented to Virginia, and the SAR Traveling Banner was presented to Indiana.

☆ The incoming National President, Rodney H. C. Schmidt, and Senior National President, Mrs. Fred W. Krueger, were elected and installed.

1974–1976

National President 1974 – 1975	Senior National President 1974 – 1976

Rodney H. C. Schmidt *Alexandria, Virginia*	**Mrs. Fred W. Krueger** *Roswell, New Mexico*

☆ National Theme: Your Government—Your Responsibility

☆ National Project: Funds for the N.S.C.A.R. Bicentennial

☆ Statement of Policy for the Operation of Regions and Regional Meetings was amended June 3, 1974.

☆ Alabama State Society had a program on "American Music" prepared and presented by a local Montgomery High School Music Department.

☆ Delaware pledged $1,000 to the C.A.R. Museum Fund. They sold Bicentennial Place Mats and Blue Hen Chickens paper weights.

☆ Nevada State C.A.R. planted 100 Evergreen trees.

☆ On December 6, 1974, the Senior National Board of Management authorized a Promotional button for twenty-five cents to be sold at Annual Convention.

☆ In commemoration of the forthcoming Bicentennial, an unique exhibit, *Sketches of New Mexico*, has been placed in the National Society Children of the American Revolution Museum. Depicting the history and culture of the Southwest, the sixty-seven item display will remain at C.A.R. National Headquarters until October 1975.

Items from the exhibit featured on the cover of the April issue of the *Daughters of the American Revolution Magazine* are Santo (image of a saint) of San Jose by Jose Benito Ortega; San Ilefonse Pueblo black on black jar made by Tonita Raybel; Yucca ring basket, used for winnowing grain, made at Jamez Pueblo; and a Navajo rug.

☆ *The Director of the National Museum of History and Technology*
and the Postmaster General
cordially invite you to attend a Philatelic Dedicatory Lecture
CONTRIBUTORS TO THE CAUSE,
by Dr. Lillian B. Miller, Historian of American Culture,
National Portrait Gallery, and
Mr. Rodney H. C. Schmidt, National President,
The National Society of the Children of the American Revolution
Tuesday afternoon, the twenty-fifth of March at 3:30 o'clock
in The Leonard Carmichael Auditorium
National Museum of History and Technology
Constitution Avenue at Fourteenth Street, Northwest, Washington City
Please reply by the enclosed card   Please present this invitation
Guests must be present by 3:15 p.m.,
otherwise seats will be given to those without Invitations

The four Contributors to the Cause postage stamps are:

8¢ Sybil Ludington
Youthful Heroine

10¢ Salem Poor
Gallant Soldier

10¢ Haym Salomon
Financial Hero

And

18¢ Peter Francisco
Fighter Extraordinary

☆ The incoming National President, Michelle Bradford Loughery, was elected and installed.

National President
1975 – 1976

Michelle Bradford Loughery
McLean, Virginia

☆ National Theme: The Time Is Now

☆ National Project: $150 of the monies go for the Special Membership Contest prize of $100 and campaign material of $50 and the balance be placed in the Museum Fund for the purchase of artifacts to support the Bicentennial Project

☆ On June 2, 1975, the Little Muddy Society, C.A.R., Cedar Rapids, Iowa, was asked to perform during the Bicentennial, by the American Bicentennial Committee. They presented an original play entitled: *Betsy Ross Makes The Flag*.

☆ Members of the Colonel Alexander Spotswood Society, Richmond, Virginia, distributed 2,000 seedlings throughout schools in the Richmond area.

☆ At the October 10 meeting of the Senior National Board of Management, permission was granted to establish a special committee to study and evaluate all aspects of the *Children of the American Revolution Magazine* for the period beginning with the March 1974 issue to date; said committee to report with recommendations to the February 1976 meeting. The

Statement of Policy for the Operation of Regions and Regional Meetings was amended.

☆ On December 5, the Senior National Board of Management confirmed the action taken by the Advisory Board to establish a special committee for the purpose of raising money to erase the Magazine deficit and to establish long-term sustaining fund for the *Children of the American Revolution Magazine*.

☆ At the February 2, 1976, meeting of the Senior National Board of Management, the Code of Behavior Rules for N.S.C.A.R. Functions was adopted. The names of the National and Senior National Officers and Chairmen are to be printed in each June issue of the *Children of the American Revolution Magazine*.

☆ The Convention honored the Bicentennial of the United States of America—1976.

☆ The incoming National President, Stephen Scott Miller, and Senior National President, Mrs. Charles M. Scheer, were elected and installed.

1976–1978

National President	Senior National President
1976 – 1977	1976 – 1978

Stephen Scott Miller	**Mrs. Charles M. Scheer**
Victoria, Texas	*Washington, D.C.*

☆ National Project: Emphasis on membership and magazine and monies be allocated as follows: Special Membership Campaign Prize $100, and balance to create a permanent fund, Special Funds, to be known as N.S.C.A.R. Magazine Sustaining Fund

☆ On June 3, 1976, the Senior National Board of Management approved a Special Magazine Committee to study the composition and content of the *Children of the American Revolution Magazine* for the purpose of creating reader interest. Both a member and senior committee are to be appointed and report its recommendations.

☆ The Regional Meetings format of panel presentations and skits was initiated to replace previous group discussion format.

☆ The Colonial Herb Garden behind the Yorktown Customhouse was established by the Moore House Society, C.A.R., in 1976 to commemorate the 200th anniversary of America's independence. When digging up the soil, many pieces of old pottery, china and glass were discovered. Several pieces have been determined to date back to the 18th century.

☆ Mrs. John Morrison Kerr, National President from 1939 to 1941, passed away on August 23, 1976.

☆ Tennessee C.A.R. members attended the Dedication Day at Kate Duncan Smith DAR School on October 26, 1976. Julie Lockert, State President, presented a check in the amount of $1,000 to be used to buy laboratory equipment for the science lab at the school. This was the first time that a C.A.R. member had ever had an active part in such a program.

☆ In February, an Acquisitions Committee was established for the purpose of purchasing artifacts for the Museum.

☆ The guidelines for and the establishment of the post of Associate Editor for the *Children of the American Revolution Magazine* was approved and the Fifth Edition of the *C.A.R. Handbook* was printed.

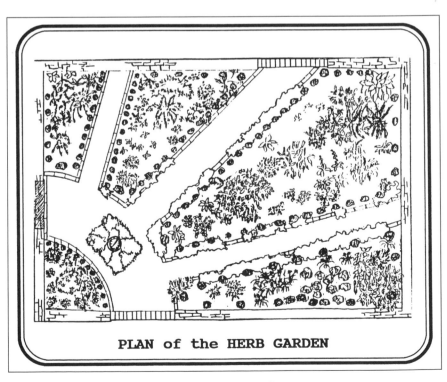

PLAN of the HERB GARDEN

Colonial Herb Garden
Yorktown, Virginia

☆ The C.A.R. opened an exhibit during DAR Continental Congress, *Patchwork of Early American Life*, in twelve newly designed cases, continuing its educational program of showing objects found in everyday life in the Colonial and Federal American periods.

☆ The incoming National President, Holly Jane Humphrey, was elected and installed.

National President
1977 – 1978

Holly Jane Humphrey
Whitewater, Wisconsin

☆ National Theme: THIS LAND—YOUR LAND

☆ National Project: Emphasis on our Nation's Wildlife Habitat with the monies going to the Magazine Sustaining Fund with the exception of $300 for subscriptions to the Ranger Rick Magazine—one to each state for one year to a school or library

☆ Since the magazine had been revised into a much less expensive form and would remain so until finances permit a return to an increased format, a committee was formed for the purpose of obtaining money for the Magazine Fund. Mrs. J. O. Miller, Victoria, Texas, was named Chairman, Magazine Fund Committee. The committee initiated the "300" Club which entitled one to wear a special pin for a $100 donation. Only 300 pins were made and each one had a number on the back for identification.

☆ For the first time in the history of the SAR, pages and aides from the C.A.R. were used at its National Congress. Several members of the Wisconsin Society served in these capacities in Milwaukee. The highlight was being interviewed and having pictures taken by the *Milwaukee Journal* which featured the C.A.R. on the front page of the Local News.

☆ An American Flag was presented to the New Children's Hospital by the District of Columbia State Society C.A.R. Cards with the Pledge of Allegiance to the Flag and the American's Creed were given out to the patients.

☆ Letters of appreciation on behalf of the National Society were endorsed for Mr. John M. Kerr for the contribution of the portrait of Mrs. William Pouch, for Mrs. John W. Finger for her contribution over the years of the National President's Award and to Mrs. Lawrence Everhart for the flame stitch chair seat for a chair in Moore House.

☆ The Committee established to study the feasibility of a suitable grave marker for deceased adults reported that such a marker could be obtained.

☆ The incoming National President, William H. Rardin, III, and Senior National President, Mrs. Stanleigh Swan, were elected and installed.

1978–1980

National President 1978 – 1979	Senior National President 1978 – 1980

William H. Rardin, III
Point Pleasant, West Virginia

Mrs. Stanleigh Swan
Alexandria, Virginia

☆ National Theme: A PAST TO REMEMBER—A FUTURE TO MOLD

☆ National Project: Funds to St Mary's School for Indian Girls to purchase biological models

☆ The Florida State Society, C.A.R., presented an historic marker to the City of Orlando containing its history and dedicated it near the lake at Eola Park on July 27, 1978. The C.A.R. emblem is at the head of the marker.

☆ Mrs. John Whelchel Finger, Senior National President from 1958 to 1960, passed away on September 22, 1978.

☆ On October 16, the Senior National Board of Management approved the recommendation that all monies in the Allen Memorial Fund on January 1, 1979, would be used to purchase an artifact for the C.A.R. Museum.

☆ Each year the President of one of the major patriotic organizations in the United States presides at the ceremonies commemorating the Anniversary of the Victory at Yorktown which occurred on October 19, 1781. This year, on the 197th anniversary, the National President of the C.A.R., William H. Rardin, III, was the presiding officer.

C.A.R. members and seniors observed the Memorial Wreath-laying Ceremony at the Monument to the Alliance and Victory and proceeded to the Battlefield where the military parade passed in review accompanied by the United States Continental Army Band of Fort Monroe, Virginia.

☆ The New Mexico State Society, C.A.R., presented a state flag to the International Space Hall of Fame. During the tour, members saw rocks that their senator brought back from the moon.

☆ The Magazine Fund Committee was authorized to purchase pins in a design approved by the Senior National President and two members of her Cabinet; the funds for same to be provided from the Magazine Fund. Authorized pins will be provided those persons making a minimum contribution of $100 to the Magazine Sustaining Fund.

☆ A special exhibition of Chinese export silver was on loan to the N.S.C.A.R. Museum from the DAR collection. It illustrated the variety of craftsmanship demonstrated by the Chinese silversmith from circa 1830 to 1875.

☆ During the 88th Continental Congress of DAR, Mrs. George U. Baylies, President General, NSDAR, remarked:

"The Children of the American Revolution, whom you will meet a little later this evening, are also bright rays of hope throughout their formative years in this organization and as they enter the ranks of the DAR. Their futures are being molded as they grow to maturity and join together with us as they leave the C.A.R. and enter the DAR and SAR."

☆ The incoming National President, Charla Ann Borchers, was elected and installed.

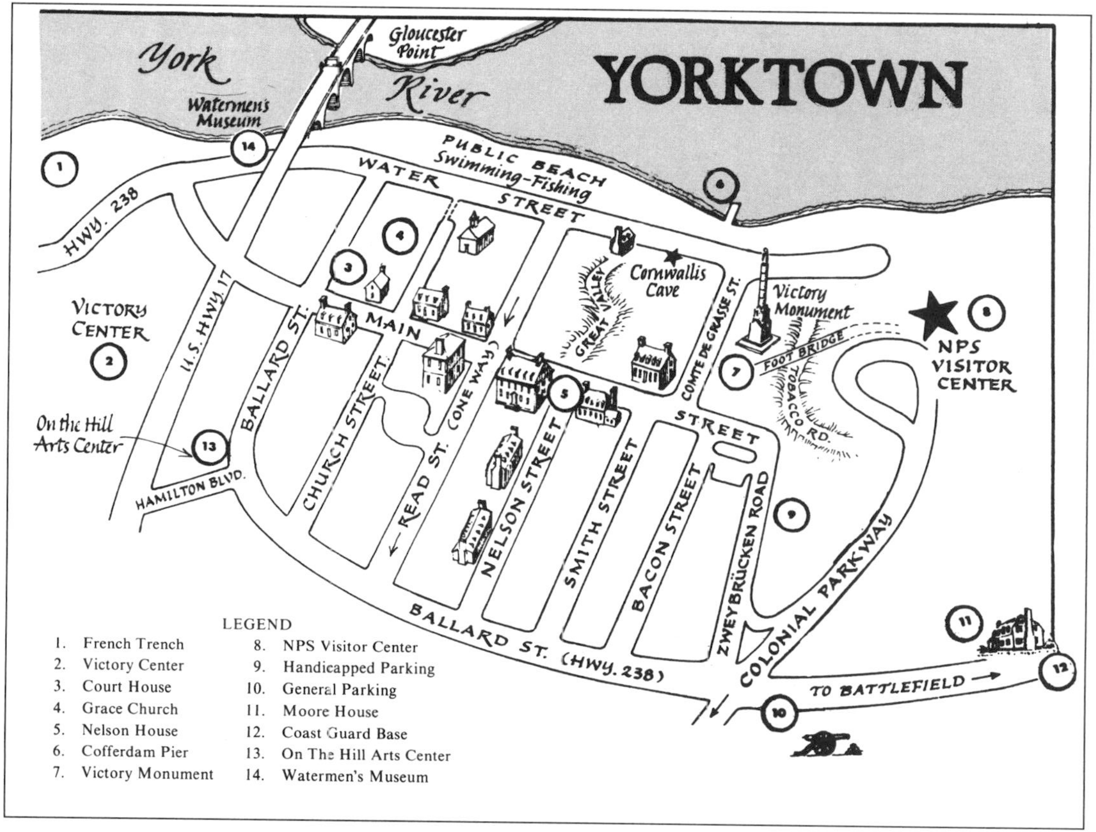

YORKTOWN
York River
Gloucester Point
Watermen's Museum
PUBLIC BEACH Swimming-Fishing
WATER STREET
HWY. 238
U.S. HWY 17
VICTORY CENTER
On the Hill Arts Center
HAMILTON BLVD.
BALLARD ST.
MAIN
CHURCH STREET
READ ST. (ONE WAY)
NELSON STREET
SMITH STREET
BACON STREET
GREAT VALLEY
Cornwallis Cave
COMTE DE GRASSE ST.
Victory Monument
FOOT BRIDGE
TOBACCO RD.
STREET
ZWEYBRÜCKEN ROAD
COLONIAL PARKWAY
NPS VISITOR CENTER
BALLARD ST. (HWY. 238)
TO BATTLEFIELD
LEGEND
1. French Trench
2. Victory Center
3. Court House
4. Grace Church
5. Nelson House
6. Cofferdam Pier
7. Victory Monument
8. NPS Visitor Center
9. Handicapped Parking
10. General Parking
11. Moore House
12. Coast Guard Base
13. On The Hill Arts Center
14. Watermen's Museum

Map of Yorktown, Virginia

National President
1979 – 1980

Charla Ann Borchers
Victoria, Texas

☆ National Theme: CARing For America

☆ National Project: Funds for the Virginia Coast Reserve and the Santa Cruz Island Preserve of the Nature Conservancy for the purpose of helping establish mainland interpretive centers in connection with each preserve.

☆ At the June 5 Senior National Board of Management, the Code of Ethics for C.A.R. National Elections was amended to read: "Campaign speeches must be delivered without the aid of posters, signs, musical instruments, or props of any description and with no reference to the opposing candidates."

☆ On June 14, at a Flag Day Celebration, Ohio's Honorary State President, Cyndy Bush, presented a check for $600 to Lagonda DAR Chapter to be used for landscaping Pennsylvania House as it appeared early in 1800. The chapter in turn presented Cyndy with a Certificate of Appreciation in recognition of the Ohio State C.A.R. contribution.

☆ On October 12, the C.A.R. gave a dinner at the Capital Hilton honoring the President General of the Daughters of the American Revolution, Mrs. George Upham Baylies. The dinner was attended by members of the

DAR National Board, DAR National Chairmen, interested DAR members and C.A.R. members and Senior Leaders.

☆ Society Activities:

Casper Collins Society, Casper, Wyoming, had excellent publicity in two newspapers, about 100 inches, and a half hour interview at a radio station.

Cherokee Rose Society, Atlanta, Georgia, gave a program of Christmas Carols and poems for the residents of Calvert Court, a home for retired Senior Citizens.

Col. Alexander Spotswood Society, Richmond, Virginia, was invited to be the choir on the 205th Anniversary of Patrick Henry's speech at an Evening Prayer Service on March 23, 1980, at historic St. John's Church in Richmond.

☆ On April 24, 1980, the Senior National Board of Management adopted the report of the Committee for the Purpose of Reviewing the Guidelines for the work of the Editors of the *Children of the American Revolution Magazine.*

☆ The Annual National Convention was the 85th Anniversary Celebration of N.S.C.A.R. A "Parade of Presidents," of seventeen Honorary National Presidents processed into the opening session of the meeting. The banquet procession also included a "parade of eight Honorary Senior National Presidents as honored guests.

National Presidents attending the Awards Banquet to celebrate the 85th anniversary were:

Lyons Mills Howland	Sharon Kay Krueger Lusk
Robert Carroll Barr	Lance David Ehmcke
Linda Lange Senf	Jane-Elizabeth Hardy
Thomas Edward Senf	Philip Field Horne
Elizabeth Bennett Campaigne	Rodney H. C. Schmidt
Van R. H. Sternbergh	Michelle B. Loughery Moss
Susan Hollingsworth Lewis	Stephen Scott Miller
Jane Wells Freeny Keegan	William H. Rardin, III
Thomas Walter Scott	

The Honorary Senior National Presidents who attended were:

Mrs. Louise Moseley Heaton	Mrs. Robert S. Hudgins
Mrs. Charles Carroll Haig	Mrs. Roy D. Allan
Mrs. Edwin H. Tiemeyer	Mrs. Fred W. Krueger
Mrs. Byron M. Vanderbilt	Mrs. Charles M. Scheer

Mrs. Lothrop, portrayed by C.A.R. member, Priscilla Bruffey, dressed in the original ball gown from the N.S.C.A.R. archives, made a surprise appearance and addressed the session.

The Awards Banquet was initiated with the recognition of contest winners, presentation of pins and traveling banners at the banquet for the first time.

☆ The Traveling DAR Banner went to Pennsylvania and the SAR Banner went to Georgia.

☆ The incoming National President, Bradley A. Bartol, and Senior National President, Mrs. Thomas G. Burkey, were elected and installed.

1980–1982

National President 1980 – 1981	Senior National President 1980 – 1982

Bradley A. Bartol
Warsaw, Indiana

Mrs. Thomas G. Burkey
Chambersburg, Pennsylvania

☆ National Theme: Believing in U.S.

☆ National Project: The purchase of a plaque for the Barn at The Wayside, Concord, Massachusetts—$200—balance to Kate Duncan Smith and Tamassee DAR Schools for General Fund

☆ The Annual Convention was held in the Sheraton Washington Hotel (formerly Sheraton Park Hotel).

☆ In the C.A.R. Museum, a representative selection from the Fred C. Bartol Collection of pre-historic American Indian Artifacts was our most important exhibition. The BARTOL COLLECTION, from Indiana, featured stone artifacts from the ADELA (1000 B.C. to A.D. 200 or 300) and HOPEWELL (400 B.C. to A.D. 300 or 400) cultures. These two overlapping cultures inhabited what we now call the Ohio Area which consists of northern Kentucky, Ohio, Indiana and southern Michigan. Included in the exhibit were examples of BANNERSTONES, GORGES, BOAT STONES, PLUMMETS, and a remarkable group of FLINT DRILLS. Of special interest is a large collection of rare TURKEY TAILS.

☆ From the office of the President General, Mrs. George Upham Baylies, is the following:

> "During the three years of this administration, promotion of the National Society Children of the American Revolution has been one of my prime interests. This fine organization instills in our young people a feeling of pride in God, Home and Country. Having been a member myself, makes all that I have tried to accomplish for these devoted young people so much more meaningful personally."

☆ On June 3, the Senior National Board of Management approved of minimum refunds of $3.00 of all monies sent to National Headquarters unless the materials requested are not available.

☆ In Concord, Massachusetts, on June 22, the N.S.C.A.R. dedicated a plaque at The Wayside, the home of our founder, Mrs. Harriett Lothrop. That Sunday was the 100th Anniversary of the publishing of Mrs. Lothrop's book, *The Five Little Peppers*, under her pen name, Margaret Sidney.

☆ Society Activities:

> Delaware State Society entered its patriotic float honoring the 203 years of the flag in the three-hour long DelMarVa[4] Chicken Festival Parade.

> Pere Marquette Society, Marshall, Michigan, beautified a local toll road marker by planting a flowerbed and took care of a special friend, Beauregard, (a skunk!) at Binder Park Zoo.

> Gov. James Thompson of Illinois proclaimed the week of August 4-9 as Illinois C.A.R. Week. Members from all over the state joined together for a week of fun-filled activities to show the state that the Land of Lincoln is Believing in U.S.

☆ At the October 6, Senior National Board of Management, authorization was given for a committee to review all slide programs of the National Society, and for a committee to review the number of Regions and geographical distribution of states within same and to consider the need for change.

On December 2, the Senior National Board of Management accepted the recommendation of the committee that reviewed the number of

[4]Combination of Delaware, Maryland, and Virginia.

Regions and the geographical distribution of states in same that there was no valid reason for changing the number of Regions and that the present distribution of States within same is satisfactory.

☆ On January 25, 1981, the Harriett M. Lothrop Society, D.C., had a Balloon Launch in honor of the released United States' hostages who were held in Iran for 444 days. Fifty-two yellow balloons were set off in honor of the hostages, along with many red and blue balloons in honor of C.A.R. Attached to each balloon was a card which bore the slogan C.A.R. Goes FAR and on the back was the society's name with addresses where people could send for more information.

☆ On February 9, at the Senior National Board of Management authorization was given to appropriate $2,500 from the Museum Fund to cover all expenses to prepare ten identical sets of slides with printed narration for the C.A.R. Museum slide program. Permission was given to the State of Oklahoma to have book plates printed using the C.A.R. Insignia to be used only in books to be presented to Kate Duncan Smith DAR School Library as part of the State Project.

☆ In February 1981, Mrs. Samuel Shaw Arentz, National President 1931 to 1932, passed away.

☆ On April 21, 1981, the Senior National Board of Management gave authorization to charge a fee for the distribution of the C.A.R. Museum Slide Program which would be available after June l.

☆ The incoming National President, Mary Sue Piacesi, was elected and installed.

National President
1981 – 1982

Mary Sue Piacesi
Washington, D.C.

☆ National Theme: PROUD, PATRIOTIC AND PROMISING
☆ National Project: In conjunction with the National Park Service, provide items for the family parlor at the Moore House, located at Colonial National Historical Park, Yorktown, Virginia
☆ Authorization was given to the Senior National President to expend funds not in excess of $1,300 from the Moore House Fund for the purpose of purchasing items for the family parlor at Moore House.
☆ At the June 1 Senior National Board of Management, approval was given for the cleaning of the draperies and carpet in the C.A.R. Board Room and the purchase of two secretary chairs for Headquarters; and that all National pins and awards to be presented at Regional Meetings shall be presented by the National President.
☆ The first audiovisual museum program developed by the C.A.R. was completed. There are thirty 35mm color slides with a printed script to interpret each artifact.
☆ Society Activities:

Canoe Creek Society, Pell City, Alabama, presented a program on Odd Facts About Our Presidents to its sponsoring DAR Chapter.

Allen Howard Society, Lilburn, Georgia, presented a program on the history of different flags of the U.S. to a SAR Chapter.

Hungerford Resolves Society, Potomac, Maryland, compiled its own book called Teens of the American Revolution. The booklet tells the true stories of teenage girls and boys who helped to win American Independence.

☆ At the October 15 Senior National Board of Management, authorization was given for a committee to be appointed to evaluate and make recommendations regarding Regional Meetings; and approval was given of the emergency action taken by the Senior National President to provide security measures in the C.A.R. Museum.

☆ October 1981 marked the 200th Anniversary of the British surrender at Yorktown and the N.S.C.A.R. was a Benefactor of the NSDAR Yorktown Bicentennial Committee.

☆ The price of individual engrossed Membership Certificates was set at $13.50 each.

☆ The DAR Traveling Banner went to Illinois; the SAR Banner to Ohio, and the S.R. Banner to Illinois and New York.

☆ The incoming National President, Gregory Kenton Barnett, and Senior National President, Mrs. Thomas H. Conner, were elected and installed.

1982–1984

National President 1982 – 1983	Senior National President 1982 – 1984

Gregory Kenton Barnett
Cynthiana, Kentucky

Mrs. Thomas H. Conner
Edina, Minnesota

☆ National Theme: PATRIOTIC MAINTENANCE: Founded in the Past! Building in the Present! Insuring the Future!

☆ National Project: The financial support of "A Legacy Preserved" and the "Mount Vernon Capital Fund."

"A Legacy Preserved" is the project to repair the DAR buildings in Washington, D.C. "The Mount Vernon Capital Fund" is the project to support the Mount Vernon Mansion and estate, home of George Washington.

☆ In May, the Wisconsin Society, C.A.R., and the Richard Newsom-Gershem Noyes Chapter, DAR, met in the woods at the intersection of Highways 26 & 60 in Dodge County to clean up a cemetery in order to find the grave of Revolutionary soldier, Gershem Noyes.

☆ The June 4 Senior National Board of Management approved the recommendation of the committee investigating information on charters that the cost of the C.A.R. Charter be increased to $60.00, and authorized the purchase of one IBM Selectric III Typewriter for Headquarters.

☆ Since the "300" Club pin was initiated in 1977 to obtain money for the Magazine to enable it to return to an increased format, it became apparent that additional funds were needed so the "300+" Pin was authorized.

☆ Society Activities:

First Free School Society, Dedham, Massachusetts, learned how to yodel as a form of communication.

Col. William Cray Society, Jacksonville, North Carolina, watched a revolutionary reenactment group and were taught to fire the musket.

Michigan State project was the hanging of an old school bell stored in the old school house on the grounds of the Moses Wisner estate in Pontiac. Governor Wisner came to Michigan in 1837; was Governor in 1859-1860; raised a regiment of infantry—mostly from Oakland County, took his men to Kentucky where he died. His remains are interred in Pontiac.

The University of North Carolina's Wilson Library asked the North Carolina State Society for copies of its state newssheet, The Tar Heel Tattler, for inclusion as a permanent part of its collection.

☆ The October 15, Senior National Board of Management authorized the purchase of one four-drawer legal size cabinet for the Genealogical Office and denied the request that the C.A.R. Insignia be used on ceramic pieces.

☆ On December 3, the Senior National Board of Management amended the Code of Behavior, Rules for N.S.C.A.R. Functions by adding a section to read, "It is illegal to stay in the function hotel without being registered with the hotel."

☆ The incoming National President, Katherine Gertrude Kennedy, was elected and installed.

National President
1983 – 1984

Katherine Gertrude Kennedy
Dayton, Ohio

☆ National Theme: GROWING TOWARD THE FUTURE

☆ National Project: To provide funds to enable St. Mary's School for Indian Girls to purchase a copying machine.

☆ On June 3, the Senior National Board of Management approved N.S.C.A.R.'s participation in the Treaty of Paris activities in Paris, France, as invited by the NSDAR; that a maximum of $150.00 be authorized to support the Treaty of Paris activities in France; approved that one adding machine be purchased for the Bookkeeper, said equipment to be purchased from the Equipment Fund; That the four surplus manual typewriters located in National Headquarters be sold as is on a carry out basis at a price to range from $15.00 to $25.00. If said typewriters are not sold by October 1, 1983, said typewriters to be given away; that the Senior National President and the Headquarters Chairman be authorized to sell the Oriental Rug, either by private sale or public auction, after consideration of expert appraisal.

☆ Society Activities:

Elisha Battle Society, Fort Worth, Texas, planted a tree near the grave of a local pioneer, William Boone, for the 107th anniversary of his settlement.

Members of the Pennsylvania State Society were able to send 5 audio nerf balls, 2 audio cricket markers, and 1 audio horse shoe pitch set to the Park View School for Blind Indian Children in Muskogee, Oklahoma, by special fund-raising attempts.

☆ The October 17 Senior National Board of Management adopted revisions to the Code of Behavior, Rules for N.S.C.A.R. Functions: "All Persons are to obey the laws of the jurisdiction in which the function is being held and the laws of the United States of America, specifically laws concerning alcohol and drugs;" and approved that due to lack of funds, small and medium sized C.A.R. flags not be purchased at this time for resale to local and state societies.

☆ On December 2, the Senior National Board of Management amended the Personnel Practices, under Rules and Regulations for Employees, Section 4, Holidays, "The following holidays shall be observed with full pay:", add "Martin Luther King's birthday—January 15".

☆ On April 19, the Senior National Board of Management amended the Bylaws and raised dues from $6.00 to $8.00.

☆ The DAR Traveling Banner went to Illinois; the SAR Traveling Banner went to Alabama, New York, South Dakota, Texas and Virginia; and the S.R. Traveling Banner went to Tennessee.

☆ The incoming National President, Samuel Walton Huddleston, II., and Senior National President, Mrs. Howard R. Kuhn, were elected and installed.

1984–1986

National President
1984 – 1985

Senior National President
1984 – 1986

Samuel Walton Huddleston, II
Virginia Beach, Virginia

Mrs. Howard R. Kuhn
Alexandria, Virginia

☆ National Theme: KEY TO THE FUTURE

☆ National Project: To contribute funds to the Statue of Liberty—Ellis Island Foundation.

☆ In 1984, forty-three states had societies.

☆ Mrs. James T. Golden, Jr., Colorado Senior State President, C.A.R., initiated the creation of a panoramic display of the history of the Smoky Hill Trail and other historical events by placement of four large interpretive panels in the Cherry Creek State Park at the Smoky Hill Trail Pavilion. This was completed in conjunction with the Colorado Park Service and the Cherry Creek Valley Historical Society.

☆ Society activities:

Georgia State Society's project is the continued support of Meadow Garden, and the contribution of funds to Georgia's Coastal Museum for the purchase of an Historical Marker.

West Virginia State Society will continue placing copies of the Flag Code in every classroom in West Virginia.

Each member of the John Augustine Washington Society, Martinsburg, West Virginia, pledged to save 100 pennies for the Statue of Liberty.

Pottowatomi Society, Milwaukee, Wisconsin, had a camp-out to visit an historic site.

Local police authorities agreed to fingerprint D.C.C.A.R. and their guests without charge. The fingerprints are kept by the parents to protect privacy.

☆ DAR SCHOLARSHIPS AVAILABLE TO C.A.R. MEMBERS

The Lillian and Arthur Dunn Scholarship in the amount of $1,000 annually for four years of college is awarded each year to eight sons or daughters of active DAR members. The applicant must be a graduating senior from an accredited high school and must plan to continue his or her education the next semester at a college or university in the United States.

The Enid Hall Griswold Memorial Scholarship in the amount of $1,000 is awarded annually to a junior or senior student attending an accredited college or university in the United States, majoring in Political Science, History, Government or Economics. Recipient must be an American citizen and must provide a transcript of grades of previous semester classes.

☆ The October 15 Senior National Board of Management, authorized a committee to study disposition of Uniform Coat of the War of 1812 and report to December 1984 meeting of the Senior National Board of Management, and authorized that upon maturity funds in Certificate of Deposit for Magazine Sustaining Fund and Life Promoters Account be increased.

☆ On December 3, the Senior National Board of Management granted extension of time until February meeting of Senior National Board of Management to report on disposition of Uniform Coat of the War of 1812.

☆ The February 4 Senior National Board of Management approved the retention of the Uniform Coat of the War of 1812 in the C.A.R. Museum Collection, and denied the request of Tennessee State Society to sell pins outside the State of Tennessee or at Regional Meetings.

☆ Mrs. Walter Hughey King, President General, NSDAR, and Mrs. Richard Powell Taylor, National Chairman NSDAR School Committee, invited the participation of C.A.R. in a special evening concert to benefit the DAR Schools.

☆ The DAR and SAR Traveling Banner went to Virginia.

☆ The incoming National President, Marie Eleanor Perkins, was elected and installed.

National President
1985 – 1986

Marie Eleanor Perkins
Kettering, Ohio

☆ National Theme: AIM FOR ACHIEVEMENT

☆ National Project: Raising Funds to computerize National Headquarters

☆ On June 7, the Senior National Board of Management approved selling of National President's theme buttons at Regional Meetings for fifty cents with money going to the National Project; denied the request of Delaware State Society to sell State Pins at Regional Meetings; denied the request of Florida State Society to sell Molly Pitcher pitchers and American Revolution Dolls at Regional Meetings; and authorized the Senior National

President to appoint a committee to study the feasibility of selling items at Regional Meetings.

☆ Society activities:

Blue Hens Chicken Society, Wilmington, Delaware, celebrated Smokey Bear's birthday with a "Teddy Bear" picnic. It was Smokey's 40th birthday and everyone arrived toting a bear of some sort.

Alexander McNair Society, St. Louis, Missouri, had an article about all the facts of the Gateway Arch.

Lady Maryland Foundation is constructing a seventy-two foot pungy schooner that will serve as a "living classroom" for Maryland Students. The Maryland C.A.R. plans to help the Lady Maryland by promoting the project and contributing financially.

☆ On October 11, the Senior National Board of Management authorized removal of St. Mary's School for Indian Girls from National Merit Award requirements for 1985-1986; authorized a committee to consider continued support of St. Mary's School for Indian Girls and report to February Board, and authorized a committee to consider possible future fund raising activities for computerization of C.A.R. National Headquarters and report to February Board.

☆ St. Mary's School for Indian Girls has been renamed St. Mary's Episcopal School, Inc. It is now operating as a coed school for boys and girls of any race, creed, color or national origin.

☆ On February 3, the Senior National Board of Management approved extension of time for committee on St. Mary's Episcopal School, Inc. to report until April Board Meeting; reaffirmed current policy of not allowing sales by states at Regional Meetings; and denied the request of Mrs. Holly Edwards Lewis to establish a national essay contest.

☆ On April 17, the Senior National Board of Management approved the continued support of St. Mary's Episcopal School, Inc. under the American Indians Committee and returned it to the National Merit Award.

☆ Mrs. Paul M. Niebell, Sr., Senior National Organizing Secretary, initiated the idea of having foldover notes and envelopes with C.A.R. insignia and received the approval of the Senior National Board to have them printed. They are wrapped ten to a package and will sell for $3.18. The first one was presented to the National President.

☆ The SAR Traveling Banner went to Iowa.

☆ The incoming National President, Eric D. Radwick, and Senior National President, Mrs. Robert Lorenzo Boggs, were elected and installed.

1986–1988

National President 1986 – 1987	Senior National President 1986 – 1988

Eric D. Radwick *Litchfield, Connecticut*	**Mrs. Robert Lorenzo Boggs** *Statesville, North Carolina*

☆ National Theme: MAKE IT HAPPEN

☆ National Project: To provide funds for Computerization of National Headquarters.

☆ On June 3, the Senior National Board of Management approved a Special Fund Raiser for computerization of Headquarters and approved an appointment of a committee of members and seniors by the National President and Senior National President to raise funds for the same, and approved the appointment of a committee by the Senior National President to study the future development of the C.A.R. Magazine; said committee to report to the February 1987 Board Meeting.

☆ Society Activities:

Members of the Savage Grant Society, Ceredo, West Virginia, laid wreaths of wild flowers on graves of six Revolutionary War Soldiers on Memorial Day.

The Glass Brothers Society, Atlanta, Georgia, visited a Children's hospital on Flag Day and gave out flags, brochures on the flag, and pens and pencils.

A member of the General Daniel Morgan Society, Martinsville, Indiana, was the recipient of the Arthur and Lillian Dunn Scholarship presented by the National Society, DAR.

The South Carolina State Society purchased an attic fan for the South Carolina Cottage at Tamassee.

Bienville Society, New Orleans, Louisiana, helped sponsor and acted as hosts at the New Orleans Museum of Art during the staging of an American Art Weekend.

Pennsylvania State Society rebound books for the York Historical Society.

☆ Through the generosity of Mrs. Dan C. Rudy, Honorary Senior National Vice President of Tennessee, a silver sauce boat was acquired from the estate of Mrs. George Upham Baylies. It matches the sauce boat donated to the C.A.R. Museum in 1982 by Mrs. Baylies, Honorary President General, NSDAR.

☆ On October 10, the Senior National Board of Management confirmed the action taken by the Senior National President to remove St. Mary's School for Indian Girls from the National Merit Award and American Indian Program, and denied the request to use the C.A.R. Insignia on T-shirts and tote bags.

☆ On October 23, 1986, Robert Carroll Barr, Junior National President from 1956 to 1957, passed away.

☆ On December 8, the Senior National Board of Management approved that all deceased current and former National Officers be listed in C.A.R. Convention Memorial Service Program and a white carnation be placed in their memory by an Honorary National President or National Officer designated by current National President.

☆ On February 2, the Senior National Board of Management deferred the committee report of the *Children of the American Revolution Magazine* to the June 1987 meeting of the Senior National Board of Management, and approved the request of Martha M. Fane to have the C.A.R. emblem etched on a brass plaque to be placed on tombstone of member, Matthew Hohl.

☆ Thank you, Mrs. Fleck! Mrs. Raymond Franklin Fleck, President General, NSDAR, invited all C.A.R. members and their parents to participate at DAR Continental Congress on Thursday evening, April 23, 1987, in the "Salute to the National Society Children of the American Revolution." This was the first time since 1960 that both members of the C.A.R. and DAR have joined together in Constitution Hall during the annual Congress.

It was a great evening! Our National Officers headed by National President, Eric D. Radwick, were led down the main aisle by the C.A.R. Flag Bearer, Bob Smith, State President of Maryland. Following introduction of National Officers, the C.A.R. Band and Chorus delighted the audience with several patriotic songs. The highlight of the event was when Mrs. Fleck played the drums with the C.A.R. Band. Following the C.A.R. presentation, the United States Air Force Band and the Singing Sergeants presented a musical rendition, *We the People*. The breathtaking climax of the evening was the lowering of the huge American Flag from the ceiling, an event that normally only occurs on opening night of DAR Continental Congress and other special occasions.

Again, Thank You, Mrs. Fleck. It was a wonderful evening, and we hope to be able to do it again soon.

☆ The incoming National President, Lori Lynn Brugier, was elected and installed.

National President
1987 – 1988

Lori Lynn Brugier
Houston, Texas

☆ National Theme: C.A.R.—THE HEART OF AMERICA

☆ National Project: (1) Participate in the Living Legacy tree planting program of U. S. Bicentennial Constitution Commission, (2) Continue raising funds for the computerization of National Headquarters (3) Place special emphasis on need to increase membership.

☆ On June 5, the Senior National Board of Management approved the selling of buttons carrying the theme "C.A.R. the Heart of America" at Regional Meetings by National President; authorized the sending of a newsletter to members of the National Board and National Chairmen by the National President, said letter to be at no cost to N.S.C.A.R., and approved by Senior National President and not to duplicate material in the *Children of the American Revolution Magazine*; approved a special award of $100 for Membership Committee, said award to be privately funded, and approved sandblasting of Tomb of the Unknown Soldier of the American Revolution in churchyard of Old Presbyterian Meeting House when the Tomb fund has the needed cost of $650.

☆ As part of Lori's Regional Tour, at every regional meeting, a tree was planted in honor of C.A.R.'s National Theme, C.A.R. The Heart of America.

☆ Arian McCullough, a member of The Glass Brothers Society in Roswell, Georgia, created a calendar picturing Georgia's remaining covered bridges. The Calendars cost $5.00 and profits will be divided between a fund for bridge preservation in Georgia and the N.S.C.A.R. National Project to computerize National Headquarters. In 1987 at the Georgia DAR State Conference, Mrs. Raymond F. Fleck, President General, NSDAR, presented Arian with the NSDAR Conservation Medal.

☆ Society Activities:

Little Muddy Society, Cedar Rapids, Iowa, combined physical fitness with conservation as members walked part of the Cedar Valley Nature Trail, picking up trash as they went.

Lexington Alarm Society, Royal Oaks, Michigan, learned about printing from Revolutionary times to the present for the National Heritage project. Their newsletter articles were written by using quill pens, rubber stamps, ball point pens, typewriters, and a computer.

Presque Isle Society, Erie, Pennsylvania, participated in the re-launching ceremonies of the United States Brig Niagara which saw action during the War of 1812.

☆ On October 16, the Senior National Board of Management approved that the *Children of the American Revolution Magazine* would be increased to 8 pages and subscription rate raised to $6.00 a year, effective July 1, 1988, with a single copy costing $2.00; approved the establishment of a permanent magazine committee to be composed of five members appointed by the Senior National President, three ex-officio members, Chairman of Finance Committee, the Editor and Associate Editor of the *Children of the American Revolution Magazine* who will meet at least once a year to review financial status of the magazine to make certain it is solvent, evaluate contents and suggest improvements, and when sufficient funds are available, recommend its enlargement; approved processing fee for supplemental lineages be increased to $25.00 effective immediately; approved a Committee on Resolutions be authorized—three members to be appointed by the National President, two Senior Advisors, with veto power, be appointed by the Senior National President; resolutions to be considered must be submitted to Committee not later than January 15, 1988, and National Parliamentarian to be member ex-officio.

☆ Society Activities:

Rock Dunder Society, South Burlington, Vermont, participated in an educational program of the DAR in Essex Junction on November

14. They presented skits about the children of various presidents including Abraham Lincoln and Theodore Roosevelt.

Members of Gerard C. Brandon Society, Brandon, Mississippi, drew names of children from the nearby Baptist Children's Village at their November meeting, then brought gifts for these children to their December meeting.

☆ On November 23, 1987, Linda Tompkins Lange Senf, National President from 1959 to 1960, passed away.

☆ On December 4, the Senior National Board of Management approved the revised guidelines for the work of the Editors of the *Children of the American Revolution Magazine*; approved the guidelines for the National and Senior National Presidents for the *Children of the American Revolution Magazine*, and the alignment of States within the Regions was approved to remain the same.

☆ On February 1, the Senior National Board of Management approved the basic design concept presented by the Special Committee for the Magazine Fund Pin, size 4/8" by 5/8", with the final design based on this concept to be approved by the Senior Magazine Fund Chairman and Senior National President. A total of 500 pins is authorized. An initial order of 300 pins is authorized to be funded by pre-selling a minimum of 26 pins.

☆ The George Washington Society, D.C., gave $150 toward the purchase and planting of one cherry tree in East Potomac Park. On April 6, 1988, the National Park Service held the "Blossoms in our future" ceremony as a thank you for the donors who gave $150. The society's tree is number AN-016 which is in the vicinity of the Jefferson Memorial.

The incoming National President, Donald J. E. Molloy, and Senior National President, Mrs. Howard E. Byrne, Jr., were elected and installed.

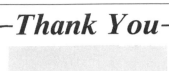

Thank You

for being a part

of the

"*Blossoms in our Future*"

ceremony

Director, National Park Service

April 6, 1988
Washington, D.C.

National Park Service

Jefferson Memorial

1988–1990

National President 1988 – 1989	Senior National President 1988 – 1990

Donald J. E. Molloy *Fort Myers, Florida*	**Mrs. Howard E. Byrne, Jr.** *Royal Oak, Michigan*

☆ National Theme: WAKE UP AMERICA—TIME FOR C.A.R.

☆ National Project: $20,000 to be raised to complete the fund for Computerization of National Headquarters.

☆ The Senior National Board of Management authorized the production of two new pins to generate funds to support the *Children of the American Revolution Magazine*. The design for the first pin includes a quill and inkwell typical of the colonial era. The pin is presented to donors contributing $100 or more to the Magazine Fund. The second pin is called the Benjamin Franklin Medallion and is a limited edition of 100. This pin features a silhouette of Benjamin Franklin and is presented to donors contributing $1000 or more to the Magazine Donor Fund.

WAKE UP AMERICA—TIME FOR C.A.R.
National Theme Button

☆ The Awards Committee met for a long energetic May weekend at the home of the Executive Secretary, Mrs. David D. Porter. At that meeting, it was decided to change the format of the Summer Information Packet. The packet had previously been loose sheets of paper, folded and packed into an envelope. The Awards Committee decided on a booklet format, which continues to the present time.

☆ From Maine to Seattle, the National Tour awakened America with a hardy *Good Morning C.A.R.* mimicking a movie of the time, *Good Morning Vietnam.*

☆ On July 15, fire completely destroyed the historic and beautiful Ohio Hobart Dining Hall at Tamassee DAR School in Tamassee, South Carolina. Six fire units responded, prevented any damage to other buildings and assured the safety of all children.

☆ Members of the Valley of Flowers Society, Bozeman, Montana, were elated when they received word from the United States Board on Geographic Names that a mountain peak in the Bridger Mountain Range would be named Naya Nuki Peak in honor of a courageous Indian girl and it would be dedicated in August, 1988.

As the story goes, a rival tribe of Indians attacked the encampment where Naya Nuki was captured. She was taken to a village over 1,000 miles away, but she noted landmarks and possible hiding places to follow home after she could escape. She survived for over a month before reaching home. The Shoshoni tribal council named her Naya Nuki which means "Girl Who Ran."

Mrs. Raymond Fleck, President General, NSDAR, with Donald J. E. Molloy, National President, N.S.C.A.R., in Lafayette Square, Washington, D.C., with the White House in the background. Donald addressed the SAR in St. John's Episcopal Church nearby.

The society members contacted the remaining members of Naya Nuki's Shoshoni tribe and they were thrilled that their ancestor was being honored by having a mountain peak named for her.

☆ On September 10, 1988, the Harriett M. Lothrop Society, D.C.C.A.R., challenged societies across the country to "TRY and raise at least $50.00 for the National Project: COMPUTERIZATION." This proved to be very successful.

☆ During Constitution Week, several societies participated in different ways:

Pierre Joseph de Favrot Society, Baton Rouge, Louisiana, presented American History posters and bulletin board items to several local schools.

In Arkansas, state C.A.R. members participated in a DAR sponsored Constitution Week luncheon and bell-ringing ceremony.

John Carroll of Carrollton Society, Howard County, Maryland, held a balloon launch (each balloon carried a message about C.A.R. and the purpose of the balloon launch) and a bell-ringing ceremony.

☆ On October 17, the Senior National Board of Management approved deletion of the title "Executive Secretary" and replaced it with "Administrator" in the N.S.C.A.R. Personnel Practices; the Senior National

President was authorized to appoint a committee of not more than five members to serve as an advisory committee on implementing the computerization of National Headquarters; and approved an amendment to the Statement of Policy for the Operation of Regions and Regional Meetings, Section "Financing," 3rd paragraph striking out $300.00 and inserting $500.00.

☆ Society Activities:

> To keep up with its members, Hallie Orme Thomas Society, Phoenix, Arizona, distributed a What's Happening? paper at each meeting for members to tell of their activities to be included in the society newsletter.

> Lexington Alarm Society, Royal Oak, Michigan, gave a play entitled Martha Washington's Dream to a local DAR Chapter. Members received rave reviews and will present it to three other DAR chapters at a future date.

> Sarah Randolph Boone Society, Vicksburg, Mississippi, members fixed a display of genealogical information and early American craft items connected with their ancestors for the Vicksburg Public Library. The display followed the theme, Our Own Ancestors Helped Make American History.

> Members of Quilna Society, Lima, Ohio, each year celebrate the meaning of Christmas by bringing gifts for the Birdcage at Crossnore. This year, in keeping with the National C.A.R. theme Wake Up America-Time for C.A.R., the society sent watches and alarm clocks.

☆ On February 6, the Senior National Board of Management approved presentation of the Franklin Medallion and Magazine Fund pin at any appropriate occasion including the Banquet at National Convention; authorized the inclusion of telephone numbers of all members of the Senior National Board of Management and Senior National Chairmen, with approval of said persons in the printed roster; and approved printing of an article in the March issue of the *Children of the American Revolution Magazine* announcing the retirement at National Convention of Mrs. David D. Porter and inviting members and seniors to come to National Convention where she would be honored.

☆ The following Message from the President of the United States of America, George H. W. Bush, was read at the Opening Night Session of the 94th N.S.C.A.R. National Convention:

> I'm pleased to extend a warm welcome to the National Society of the Children of the American Revolution as you assemble for your

annual Convention in Washington. I wish I could be there to meet you all.

As descendants of the patriots who won our nation's independence, you enjoy a proud heritage. But even more impressive than your lineage is your tremendous love for this country. You show that love when you generously aid native Americans and Appalachian children. You show that love when you work to conserve our Nation's wildlife and natural resources. You show it when you study our history and our form of government—the system of self-government for which our ancestors fought and died. It's encouraging for me to know that young people are carrying on the patriotic spirit and proud traditions that have helped make the United States of America a great Nation.

Mrs. Bush joins me in wishing you an exciting, memorable Convention.

/s/ George Bush

☆ The staff of the Sheraton Washington Hotel made a surprise presentation during the banquet to honor Mrs. David D. Porter. Waiters paraded down the stairs and into the Sheraton Ballroom with individually decorated desserts for each table. The waiters circled around the room to music, lights, and fanfare and then lined up in front of Mrs. Porter for a bow and salute to her for her twenty-eight years of working with the Hotel staff on behalf of C.A.R. The Director of Conventions for the Hotel pre-

Mrs. David D. Porter
Executive Secretary/Administrator

sented Mrs. Porter with a Waterford clock on behalf of the Sheraton Washington Hotel.

Members, seniors, and those who had known Mrs. Porter throughout her thirty-five years of service chose to honor her with a farewell salute. National President, Donald Molloy, called Mrs. Porter to the podium to take a seat while members sang *Our Fair Grace*, a musical presentation written to the tune of *I've Grown Accustomed to Her Face* from *My Fair Lady*. The National President then presented her with several gifts on behalf of the Senior National Board of Management. Senior leaders were contacted nationwide resulting in the presentation of a $1,000 Benjamin Franklin Medallion for the Magazine Fund and a check for several thousand dollars for a bon voyage retirement.

For her many years of service, Mrs. David D. Porter was "Gracefully" saluted by her many friends.

☆ The incoming National President, Elizabeth Anne Jones, was elected and installed.

National President
1989 – 1990

Elizabeth Anne Jones
Saratoga, California

☆ National Theme: C.A.R.—BUILDING BRIDGES INTO THE FUTURE
☆ National Project: (1) To obtain, maintain, and retain members for a net gain and increased interest in C.A.R. (2) Encourage societies to contribute articles, pictures, puzzles, and ideas to the National Magazine. (3) To raise funds for office furnishings in National Headquarters to complement new equipment.

C.A.R.-BUILDING BRIDGES INTO THE FUTURE
National Theme Button

☆ The Senior National Board of Management approved acceptance of a gift of two dummy boards (Revolutionary War soldier replicas) from Miss Laura E. Boice and the proposal from K & R Industries for the manufacture of Museum Major Benefactor pins (RED APPLES).

☆ Ms. Stiles Wilkins replaced Mrs. Porter as Administrator.

☆ Fraunces Tavern Society, C.A.R., New York, New York, was invited to march in the April 30, 1989 parade held in Lower Manhattan in celebration of the Bicentennial of George Washington's Inauguration. The C.A.R. contingent, placed between the S.R. and DAR, began the 3.39 mile march at precisely 1:43 p.m. Society President, Weston M. F. Almond, carried the Society flag. Members ranging in age from four to twenty were dressed in 18th century costumes loaned by the National Society Colonial Dames of America. The Procession filed past the reviewing stand where a large number of officials waved to and greeted them.

☆ Vermont State Society grew tomato plants and sold the seedling plants and tomatoes to raise funds for the National Project. Two of the younger members of Mary Wessells Society, Piedmont, California, learned to make Braille Flags and gave them to blind seniors. Alison and Lindsey Marsh's Grandmother taught them to make the stitches so the stripes and stars can be felt by the blind.

☆ On Saturday, October 14, 1989, over 1500 people gathered for the Dedication Ceremony of the Yorktown French Memorial. The Monument includes over 600 names of Frenchmen who lost their lives during the Campaign of Yorktown in 1781, including the Battle off the Virginia Capes. The names of the soldiers face the land and the sailors face the sea. Remarks were made by Colonel Stewart B. McCarty, Jr., Past State President, D.C. SAR, on behalf of the National Societies DAR and C.A.R. at the ceremony.

☆ On December 1, the Senior National Board of Management gave permission to the United States Department of the Interior, National Parks Service to change the Family Parlor to the Master Bedroom in the Moore House, Yorktown, Virginia, as per its recommendations (not to exceed $2,000.00) as stated in its letter dated September 26, 1989.

☆ Mrs. Donald Bennett Adams, National President from 1947 to 1951, passed away on December 9, 1989.

☆ On February 5, 1990, the Senior National Board of Management approved an invitation to Mrs. David D. Porter as a guest for life to all N.S.C.A.R. National Convention functions, and reaffirmed the current rule that all attendees at N.S.C.A.R. National Convention are required to pay registration fee.

☆ The Senior National Board of Management amended the Bylaws to allow Annual Convention to be held in the Metropolitan area of Washington, D.C.

☆ The *Bylaws* were reprinted in a revised format and the seventh edition of the *C.A.R. Handbook* was updated and reprinted.

☆ On April 12, 1990, the Senior National Board of Management authorized the incoming Senior National President to appoint a special study committee to review committee work and structure.

☆ The incoming National President, G. Taylor Davis, and Senior National President, Mrs. Paul Milton Niebell, Sr., were elected and installed in the hotel due to the rainy weather.

1990–1992

National President
1990 – 1991

Senior National President
1990 – 1992

G. Taylor Davis
Pinewood, South Carolina

Mrs. Paul Milton Niebell, Sr.
Potomac, Maryland

☆ National Theme: GROWING STRONG IN C.A.R.

☆ National Project: To raise funds for Tamassee DAR School for an ice cream machine

☆ On June 1, the Senior National Board of Management recommended to the Bylaws Committee to delete "at large" from Article V, Section 1 and substitute "Regional Vice Presidents;" recommended Article VII, Part B, Section B-1 be amended by adding, "The Senior National President shall have no authority to disburse any amount of the funds of the National Society without approval of the Senior National Board of Management;" and recommended Article XI, Section 4 be amended by adding a new sub-section C "National dues may be paid in advance through age 22." Also, that the N.S.C.A.R. become a member of the National Congress of Patriotic

GROWING STRONG IN C.A.R.
National Theme Button

Organizations. That National Presidents appoint chairmen for the Foreign Societies; and that the Senior National President appoint a Special Committee known as N.S.C.A.R. Centennial Committee.

☆ The Senior National Board of Management accepted the gift from Mrs. Paul M. Niebell, Sr., of two bookcases for the Senior National President's office.

☆ LIFE MEMBERSHIP

Although the opportunity to become a life member has been available for a long time, most members and seniors are unaware of it. Life membership is a very valuable tool for retaining members. Becoming a life member involves paying national dues through the year in which one turns 22 years old. Life memberships make thoughtful gifts. Encourage parents, grandparents, aunts, uncles, and friends to give life memberships for birthdays, Christmas, graduation, and other special occasions. Life membership has its privileges. Most importantly, anyone who becomes a life member gets a stylish red, white, and blue *C.A.R. Life Member* pin to wear for all occasions, particularly C.A.R. events.

☆ At the NSSAR Congress in Louisville, Kentucky, the National Presidents were invited to a lovely reception at Springfield, the boyhood home of Zachary Taylor.

☆ Society activities:

Medicine Bluff Society, Lawton, Oklahoma, decorated cards for American soldiers in Saudi Arabia

The Michigan Society sold pencils that read Michigan Society C.A.R. to raise money to help re-upholster an 1880 wing chair in the museum that was the home of former Governor Warren (1905-1911).

Life C.A.R. Member Pin

Polly Todd Society, Flint, Michigan, visited cemeteries where members placed flags on the grave sites of American Revolutionary War Soldiers and trimmed grass around the tombstones.

Captain John Ward Veazey Society, Severna Park, Maryland, presented a handmade quilt to the Maryland State Regent in honor of the DAR Centennial. The squares of the quilt were designed and embroidered by members to represent the importance of the history of the parent organization.

☆ On October 11, 1990 at the 100th Anniversary Birthday Dinner, NSDAR, a toast to the future was given by Catherine Lisle, National Librarian-Curator, for the N.S.C.A.R.

☆ The October Senior National Board of Management changed the committee named "C.A.R. Foreign Societies" to"N.S.C.A.R. Societies in Foreign Countries"; approved that Mrs. Mary Matthews of Yorktown, Virginia, be the recipient of a Benjamin Franklin Medallion for her generous contribution of $1,000; and approved that an Endowment Pin be presented to Mrs. Thurston H. Baxter as a memorial to Col. Baxter for the $1,000 contribution received from his estate.

☆ Mrs. W. Earle Hawley, Senior National President, from 1962 to 1964, passed away on October 16, 1990.

☆ YORKTOWN DAY

The C.A.R. Senior National President, along with Mrs. Eldred Martin Yochim, President General, NSDAR, the principal speaker, rode with Ms. Stiles Wilkins, C.A.R. Administrator, to Yorktown, Virginia. In the evening, they attended a lovely banquet at Fort Eustis, where the National President, G. Taylor Davis, and his mother, Mrs. S. Perry Davis, joined the festivities.

The next morning, the National Presidents were privileged to ride in the motorcade to the French Cemetery for the ceremony and wreath laying; to the French Monument in memory of French war veterans for another ceremony.

Following the parade, the National President presided at the patriotic exercises at the Monument to Alliance and Victory, and Miss Cheryl Menke, National Chaplain, was the Honorary Flag Bearer. Then, the 18th Century Tactical Demonstrations and the Old Guard Fife and Drum Corps from Fort Myer were reviewed.

During the day, Mrs. Philip W. Bernstorf, Senior National First Vice President, along with Dr. Bernstorf, Honorary Senior National Vice President, presented Mrs. Mary Matthews with her Benjamin Franklin Medallion. Mrs. Matthews remarked that public buildings look "dead" without the flags flying—that the national and state business never stops, and the flags flying at the buildings would emphasize the life and vitality of the on-going business of the government.

Following the ceremonies, Mrs. Yochim and the Senior National President flew to Tamassee, South Carolina, to present the gifts from the National Societies to Tamassee DAR School.

☆ The Suggestion Box received the following:

> Wouldn't it be nice to have the Honorary National Presidents and National Chairmen who attend Annual Convention sit at the Head Table at the Awards Banquet.

National President G. Taylor Davis presiding over Yorktown Day Celebration in October 1990

193

Dr. Philip W. Bernstorf with Mrs. Mary Matthews, owner of Nick's Seafood Restaurant, receiving her Benjamin Franklin Medallion from Mrs. Bernstorf

Since Headquarters will be closed during Annual Convention, why not sell some supplies in the Registration Booth area.

☆ On December 3, 1990, the Senior National Board of Management gave permission to purchase 1000 sets of U.S. Flag/N.S.C.A.R. Flag and black plastic bases with two holes to sell for $5.00 per set; this item would be placed on the C.A.R. order form.

☆ Mrs. Charles M. Scheer, Senior National President from 1976 to 1978, passed away on January 19, 1991.

☆ On February 4, 1991, the Senior National Board of Management approved the recommendation from the Advisory Board that the *Children of the American Revolution Magazine* be sent to the President General, NSDAR; the President General, NSSAR; and the General President, GSSR.

☆ At the opening session of the 96th Annual Convention, *Saluting the Honorary National Presidents 50th Anniversary 1941—1991*, the attendees were honored with a keynote address by The Honorable Floyd Davidson Spence, United States Congressman, South Carolina. His address dealt with American Patriotism and flag waving.

The following letter from The Honorable Strom Thurmond, United States Senate, South Carolina, was received at C.A.R. National Headquarters too late to be read at the Convention:

Dear Friends:

I would like to take this opportunity to extend my best wishes and congratulations to the National Society Children of the American Revolution on their 96th Annual Convention.

We are proud of this fine organization which contributes so much to our nation, and we are grateful for their outstanding work in promoting patriotism and upholding the principles of American Liberty.

Again, I send my congratulations...as well as my best wishes for an enjoyable and productive Convention. May God bless you and may God bless America.

With kindest regards and best wishes,

Sincerely,
/s/ Strom Thurmond

SALUTING THE HONORARY NATIONAL PRESIDENTS

The 1991 Annual Convention saluted all Honorary National Presidents on the Fiftieth Anniversary of the first Honorary National President. Twelve, an even dozen, Honorary National Presidents returned and processed in at the Saturday Night Banquet and made quite an impression seated at Head Table Two. Those attending included:

Lyons Mills Howland
the Number One Honorary "Junior"National President
Mrs. Elizabeth Prince Bennett Campaigne
Mrs. Sharon Kay Krueger Lusk
Lance David Ehmcke
Rodney H. C. Schmidt
William H. Rardin, III
Charla Ann Borchers
Bradley A. Bartol
Samuel Walton Huddleston, II
Marie Eleanor Perkins
Donald J. E. Molloy
Elizabeth Anne Jones

It was a once in a lifetime occasion and enjoyed by all.

☆ The incoming National President, Heather Love Stephens, was elected and installed.

National President
1991 – 1992

Heather Love Stephens
Dallas, Texas

☆ National Theme: OLD GLORY, NEW PRIDE
☆ National Project: Raise $5,000 for a new lunchroom office at Kate Duncan Smith DAR School at Grant, Alabama.
☆ The National President initiated a special program entitled *Kids Helping Kids*. This program was designed to encourage local societies to reach out to schools, churches, day-care centers, etc., and offer their services to those less fortunate.
☆ The reference books on antiques, donated to the Museum several years ago, by Honorary Senior National President, Mrs. Stanleigh Swan, have a new home. These rare books on antiques are from her late husband's collection. They became accessible for museum research thanks to the generosity of Senior National President, Mrs. Paul M. Niebell, Sr., who donated a much needed pair of bookcases.

OLD GLORY - NEW PRIDE
National Theme Button

☆ The glass panes in the windows in the C.A.R. museum have been painted through the years. DAR removed the paint from these windows. The beautiful, graceful fan windows greatly enhance the museum. The sunlight streamed in and made the museum much lighter and brighter. However, the textiles and paper items had to be protected from the harmful light rays. After consulting with experts, plans were made to place protective film on approximately thirty displays.

☆ On June 4, 1991, the Senior National Board of Management approved the authority to appoint a special committee consisting of three members and two seniors to investigate the possibility of producing a "Join-the-C.A.R." video; the recommendation to allow local and state societies to secure donations from companies, etc. for the sole purpose of supporting the publication of their respective C.A.R. Newsletters; that protective film be purchased for necessary exhibits in the N.S.C.A.R. Museum not to exceed $1,500; and sell the Summer Packets for $2.00, and if mailed, for $3.00.

The Senior National Board of Management also approved the sale of National Theme buttons for $1.00; National Theme decals for $1.00; and National Theme T-shirts. This was the first time T-shirts had been offered by the National Society and the T-shirts were so popular, the tradition continues today.

☆ Some of the skits used for panel presentations focused on Dr. Seuss, the popular author of children's books. Of particular interest was *The Lorax* used for the Conservation program and *The Cat in the Hat* used for membership.

The National Tree Trust donated trees which were planted at each region and this was a tremendous success. During the Regional meetings, time was devoted to planting trees for conservation and the National President developed a strong arm wielding the shovels.

Members of the Southeastern Region and the National Society planted a Palmetto tree, state tree of South Carolina, to insure our part of having been present and helping the environment for those after us.

The South Carolina State Society thanked Heather Love Stephens, National President and her Board; Mrs. James Cook, South Carolina Senior State President; the city of Charleston; the National Tree Trust and the state organization, Low Country Relief, for their assistance in making the tree planting a reality.

☆ Societies Activities

N.S.C.A.R.—We CARE About New Jersey was the theme of Matthew De Fazio, State President, 1991-1992. The restoration of President's cradle and the medallion case at the Grover Cleveland birthplace in Caldwell, New Jersey, were his state projects.

Heather Love Stephens, National President, with Mr. David S. Johnson, Senior National Vice President for Mid-Southern Region, at the tree planting ceremony in Bardstown, Kentucky

Prairie Dog Society, Wichita, Kansas, held a meeting where a veteran of Desert Storm and one of the servicemen with whom the society members corresponded, attended the meeting and told of some of his experiences in Operation Desert Shield and Desert Storm.

Fort Washington Society, Cincinnati, Ohio, as its annual membership program, held a square dance at the historic Waldschmidt House which is maintained by the Ohio Society DAR.

Members of the D.C. State Society participated in the gala 200th birthday celebration of the District of Columbia on September 7, 1991.

A "Bird Cage Birthday Party" was held by the Hallie Orme Thomas Society, Phoenix, Arizona, where members brought gifts to send to Crossnore.

☆ On October 16, the Senior National Board of Management granted permission to the N.S.C.A.R. Centennial Committee to contact the United States Postal Service to request a 100th Anniversary Commemorative Stamp, authorized said committee to conduct a nation-wide contest among C.A.R. members and senior leaders to establish a theme and a logo for the N.S.C.A.R. Centennial; authorized said committee to investigate the feasibility of having a special pin for the N.S.C.A.R. Centennial. After an open discussion at the Board Meeting, it was decided to list deceased members and seniors so the N.S.C.A.R. family would be informed through the *Children of the American Revolution Magazine.*

☆ The 1990-1991 National Project was dedicated on Founders' Day at Tamassee on October 19, 1991.

☆ On December 2, 1991, the Senior National Board of Management approved the recommendation from the Advisory Board that in case of the death of an Honorary Senior National President, the insignia may be returned to the National Society as a gift or for sale was approved.

☆ In December, the Colorado State Society decorated the door of the Danielson Sod Schoolhouse at the Plains Conservation Center built in 1966-67 as a project of the Colorado C.A.R. assisted by the Peace Pipe Chapter, NSDAR, and others. The furnished room is toured by students and children for historical and educational purposes.

☆ What a wonderful surprise! The new format for the March 1992 issue of the *Children of the American Revolution Magazine* featured National President Heather Stephens' logo on the cover. After many years of being a four page newsletter, the *Children of the Revolution Magazine* returned to a booklet format. Much credit went to the Editor, Mrs. Charles F. Decker. This was really Old Pride, New Glory!

Mrs. Paul M. Niebell, Sr., Senior National President, and G. Taylor Davis, Honorary National President, operating the "Taylor-Made" ice cream machine at Tamassee DAR School in South Carolina

☆ CONVENTION AD BOOK SUPPORTS NATIONAL CONVENTION

To save the attendees money at National Convention and to keep the cost of registration down, this year a Sponsor Booklet was printed. This booklet was distributed to everyone who attended the Awards Banquet. On each page the person or company put a greeting or message in the space. There were five choices: Full page costs—$100; Half page—$50; Quarter page—$25; Eighth page—$15; and a listing with no message—$10.

☆ The Alexandria Royal Fyfes & Drums opened the 97th Annual Convention at the Crystal Gateway Marriott Hotel in Arlington, Virginia, with a patriotic musical program.

Mrs. Raymond Franklin Fleck, Honorary President General, NSDAR, and a long-time loyal supporter of C.A.R. presented a lovely slide presentation of Harriett Mulford Lothrop to the Convention. The presentation was followed by Mrs. Fleck entertaining the children with her drum. The children are always delighted and fascinated by Mrs. Fleck's abilities on the drum, particularly when she does her special rendition of a train ride.

For the first time Installation Ceremonies took place in the George Washington Masonic National Memorial in Alexandria, Virginia.

The incoming National President, Robert D. Warren, and Senior National President, Mrs. Philip W. Bernstorf, were elected and installed.

The Alexandria Royal Fyfes and Drums who performed at the 97th Annual Convention

The George Washington Masonic National Memorial, Alexandria, Virginia

1992–1994

National President
1992 – 1993

Senior National President
1992 – 1994

Robert D. Warren
Fairfax Station, Virginia

Mrs. Philip W. Bernstorf
Wichita, Kansas

☆ National Theme: EXPLORE AMERICA with C.A.R.

☆ National Project: Restoration and stabilization of artifacts found at an archaeological dig at Mt. Vernon.

☆ Congratulations to Westland Printers, which prints the *Children of the American Revolution Magazine*. They were among twelve winners of the U. S. Postal Service's annual Quality Supplier Award, defeating 60,000 other postal contractors nationally, to be named superior in responsiveness, service, and value.

☆ Mrs. Joseph Wathen became the new Administrator replacing Ms. Stiles Wilkins. Mrs. Wathen has been in C.A.R. National Headquarters for more than twenty years and was promoted to this position.

EXPLORE AMERICA WITH C.A.R.
National Theme Button

☆ On June 1, 1992, the Senior National Board of Management approved a C.A.R. Centennial Pin design proposed by the N.S.C.A.R. Centennial Committee; the offering of the pin for $100 and $200 for a pin with a diamond; to take advance orders for 200 pins; to limit the total number of Centennial Pins by prohibiting the manufacture after December 31, 1995, and that the pin be authorized for wear on the official ribbon or separately; that the Senior National President was to proceed with procurement of funds for microfiche conversion of the Membership Applications and Supplements.

☆ Society Activities:

Six members of the Los Ninos Society, Fullerton, California, in colonial costume acted as a color guard at the dedication and opening to the public of a permanent display of a valuable copy of the Declaration of Independence at the Richard Nixon Library and Birthplace in Yorba Linda, California.

Little Mountain Society, Painesville, Ohio, planted a sapling at Bedford Reservation in Bedford. The tree had been started from a seed that came from the white oak grove of Abraham Lincoln's homestead.

Members of the Old Stage Road Society, Memphis, Tennessee, served as docents at Davies Manor, the oldest house in Shelby County. The landmark also serves as the local headquarters of the C.A.R., DAR, and SAR.

The Presidio Hill Society, San Diego-LaJolla, California, is participating in the "Penny Pines" project sponsored by the U.S. Forest Service. 6800 pennies ($68.00) will reforest one acre of burned National Forest.

✫ At the Eastern Regional held in Beltsville, Maryland, members and guests viewed some Mount Vernon artifacts and met Mr. Dennis Pogue, Chief Archaeologist, and Mr. Michael Quinn, Educational Director, from Mt. Vernon.

✫ Another happy event was when Mrs. Charles F. Decker (Vanra), Editor of the *Children of the American Revolution Magazine*, received the Benjamin Franklin Medallion Number 86 from Robert Warren, National President. Number 86 represented the first year Mrs. Decker served as Editor of the magazine.

✫ Society Activities:

> Members of the Mary Gardner Owen Society, Marietta, Ohio, dedicated a new plaque in honor of their namesake who arrived in Ohio 204 years ago.

> Members of the John Augustine Washington Society, Martinsburg, West Virginia, participated in the dedication of the relocation of the grave of Captain John Kearney, an American Revolutionary War soldier. The original burial grounds were discovered during the construction of a new shopping mall.

✫ On October 16, the Senior National Board of Management accepted the recommendation of the National Board to add to Item 6 of the Code

Robert D. Warren, National President; Mr. Dennis Pogue showing some artifacts; Mrs. Philip W. Bernstorf, Senior National President; and Mr. Michael Quinn

Mrs. Charles F. Decker receiving her Benjamin Franklin Medallion from Robert D. Warren

of Ethics: "All campaign speeches must be delivered entirely from the floor microphone," and instructed that securities held in Safe Deposit Box be removed, the lock box closed, and the rental contract terminated. The securities will be placed into street name accounts for the Endowment Fund and Finance Committee Funds.

☆ The December 4 Senior National Board of Management took action to store the works of Harriett Lothrop in an archival safe location; amended the Code of Ethics by adding the following: "Candidates may not request audience participation during their speeches;" authorized the Senior National President to enter into a Computer Support Contract at $45.00 per hour on Richard Elliott's (the computer software specialist) #2 option; and instructed the Board to have the N.S.C.A.R. Application Papers copied to a microfiche format without provisions from the budget.

☆ Mrs. Charles Carroll Haig, Senior National President from 1951 to 1955, passed away on December 15, 1992.

☆ On February 5, 1993, the Senior National Board of Management approved a New Life Member Pin to be worn on the official ribbon and produced by J. E. Caldwell & Co.; approved the increase of the *Children of the American Revolution Magazine* subscription rate to $8.00 per year and $3.00 single copy; authorized the mailing or delivery of the C.A.R.

Centennial Pins and/or their presentation at National Convention; the procurement of new flag poles where necessary and to bill the appropriate State Society.

☆ N.S.C.A.R. NEW VIDEO LIBRARY

There is now a new great program resource for local societies. Send request and rental fee of $5.00 per video tape to Senior National Treasurer, N.S.C.A.R. Some of the videos are:

The Life of George Washington
Mount Vernon—Home of George Washington
The Defense of Fort McHenry
Mystic Seaport
Virginia Plantations—Mount Vernon, Monticello
and Shirley Plantation
Washington, DC—An Inspiring Tour
Washington, DC—hosted by Willard Scott.

The short form membership applications were discontinued and short forms in circulation will be accepted ONLY until the October 1993 meeting of the Senior National Board of Management.

☆ The April 22, 1993, Senior National Board of Management approved a task force, consisting of the National Librarian-Curator, the Senior National Librarian-Curator, the Senior National President, and up to three additional members to be appointed by the Senior National President to be established to study the issues and museum property at Gadsby's Tavern, to develop a proposal for review and action by the October 1993 Senior National Board; a C.A.R. Centennial Committee to be established to develop ideas, projects and activities for the C.A.R. Centennial Celebration; said committee to dissolve automatically on May 1, 1996, unless retained by further action; a *C.A.R. Handbook* Committee be formed to revise the current Handbook with suggestions submitted by November 1, 1993, and the experimental phase of the committee structure revision process be concluded.

☆ The 98th Annual Convention was held at the Radisson Plaza at Mark Center, Alexandria, Virginia—a new location.

☆ The National President, Robert D. Warren, introduced Mr. Dennis Pogue, Chief Archaeologist at Mt. Vernon and presented him with a check for $5,000 to assist in the archaeological dig in progress at the estate, the 1992-1993 National Project. The items will be displayed in a museum case marked as being supported by the National Society Children of the American Revolution.

Mrs. Donald Shattuck Blair
President General
National Society Daughters of the American Revolution
Administration Building, 1776 D Street, N.W.
Washington, D.C. 20006-5392

May 14, 1993

Mrs. Philip W. Bernstorf
Senior National President
National Society Children of the
  American Revolution
1776 D Street, N.W.
Washington, DC 20006-5392

Dear Mrs. Bernstorf:

At its meeting April 16, 1993, the DAR Executive Committee
adopted the following:

> "...ratify the action of the President General
> in renewing the "Contract For Use Of Office
> Space" between the NSDAR and the National
> Society Children of the American Revolution.
> Said contract extends through December 1995
> with the terms remaining the same as in the
> prior contract."

A copy of this renewed contract is enclosed.

Sincerely,

Mrs. Donald Shattuck Blair

*Copy of letter dated May 14, 1993 from Mrs. Donald Shattuck Blair, President
General, NSDAR, to Mrs. Philip W. Bernstorf, Senior National President,
N.S.C.A.R.*

CONTRACT FOR USE OF OFFICE SPACE

THIS CONTRACT Made and entered into by and between the NATIONAL SOCIETY DAUGHTERS OF THE AMERICAN REVOLUTION, party of the first part, and the NATIONAL SOCIETY CHILDREN OF THE AMERICAN REVOLUTION, party of the second part,

WITNESSETH:

Party of the first part hereby gives to the party of the second part the use of the south end of the old library in Constitution Hall, being approximately two-thirds of said room for permanent headquarters, such space having dimensions of approximately 18 feet by 78 feet at one end thereof and 35 feet by 49 feet at the other end thereof.

Party of the second part agrees to pay in advance for the maintenance of the above space the sum of Two Hundred Dollars ($200) per year, payable semi-annually on May 1st and November 1st of each year and $25.00 per year for electricity payable in advance May 1st.

Party of the second part further agrees that all alterations, redecorating and repairs required in the use of the above space shall be at the expense of the party of the second part so long as this contract exists.

No structural changes shall be made except by the approval of the Executive Committee of the party of the first part.

IN WITNESS WHEREOF parties hereto have executed this Agreement by their proper officers, this 15th day of of April, 1993.

NATIONAL SOCIETY OF THE DAUGHTERS
OF THE AMERICAN REVOLUTION

_____   By _____
Recording Secretary General, NSDAR   President General, NSDAR

NATIONAL SOCIETY OF THE CHILDREN
OF THE AMERICAN REVOLUTION

By _____
Senior National President, N.S.C.A.R.

Contract Renewal with C.A.R. through December 1995.

Copy of CONTRACT FOR USE OF OFFICE SPACE between the National Society Daughters of the American Revolution and the National Society Children of the American Revolution dated April 15, 1993

☆ The incoming National President, Elizabeth Ann Lee, was elected and installed.

National President
1993 – 1994

Elizabeth Ann Lee
Louisville, Kentucky

☆ National Theme: C.A.R.: The Great Adventure
☆ National Project: To raise $5,000 for "The Wayside" at Minuteman National Park, Concord, Massachusetts, for an interpretative guidebook, a "bag of historical tricks" and a plaque clearly identifying N.S.C.A.R.'s participation.
☆ The June 1, 1993, Senior National Board of Management authorized the microfilm or microfiche recording and preservation of N.S.C.A.R. lineage records as a C.A.R. Centennial Project.
☆ Mrs. Louise Moseley Heaton, National President from 1941 to 1945, passed away on June 22, 1993.
☆ The Royal Auvergne Society, Paris, France, joined the DAR and SAR in attending the Royal Auvergne Ball and swung to rhythms from New Orleans by the 5 Dixie Stompers Band.
☆ Society Activities

C.A.R. . . . THE GREAT ADVENTURE
National Theme Button

John Morton Society, Chester, Pennsylvania, adopted a chinchilla and a sand boa at the Philadelphia Zoo.

Lexington Alarm Society, Royal Oaks, Michigan, includes book reviews in its newsletter.

Three societies in Colorado: Pikes Peak, Stegosaurus, and William Smith Livingston participated in the 100th Anniversary Celebration of the writing of America the Beautiful.

Texas State Society helped stock 1300 fish in a local pond, and is saving canceled stamps for a Rehabilitation Center in a Veterans' Hospital.

☆ The October 15 Senior National Board of Management approved the removal of partitions north of the Administrator's and Senior National President's offices and to install carpeting throughout the C.A.R. National Headquarters.

The Headquarters Committee is hard at work to renovate Headquarters offices. At least some of the work will have been accomplished by the December Board. The target date for completion is the first of the year — depending upon receiving computer furniture which has been ordered, coordination of the construction people and the electricians.

☆ At the December 2 Senior National Board of Management, authorization was given to purchase from the Equipment Fund through Ferret Software a new computer with Recordable CD drive, scanner and peripherals, a new printer and upgrades of DOS, Windows, WordPerfect, and *FoxPro*; approved the recommendation of the Headquarters Committee for the replacement of the ceiling fixtures at a cost of approximately $3,600.

☆ On February 4, 1994, at the Senior National Board of Management, approval was given for standard flag streamers to be created for awards to the three best societies in the National Society in lieu of silver bowls to begin in 1995; in addition, National Gold Merit Award winners are to be presented with Flag Streamers to begin with 1994 Convention.

☆ National Bylaws were amended to enable a member of SAR or S.R. to become the Senior National President and/or the Senior National First Vice President.

☆ The Senior National Board of Management, on April 21, authorized a revolving fund of $2,000 be established in the budget to allow the National President to plan for theme promotional sales items. Items will be approved by the Senior National Board of Management, and funds will be expended from the current fund. After the $2,000 has been returned to the Current Fund, profits will go to the National Project.

☆ At the 99th Annual Convention, the George Washington Honor Medal was presented to N.S.C.A.R. The presenter read:

> "Through a multitude of programs and activities in their communities, schools, churches and with other organizations, the N.S.C.A.R. has helped to further patriotism and love of Country, as well as, a better understanding of our rich and wonderful heritage."

☆ An interesting report was given by Carrie Susan Hults, National Chairman of N.S.C.A.R. Societies in Foreign Countries. A partial quote follows:

> ". . . The majority of the C.A.R. members do not know of the Societies overseas, let alone their names or how many members they have.
>
> "The Royal Auvergne Society in France chose its name from the regiment that received recompense for its excellent conduct in America, particularly at the siege of Yorktown. This Society is active and has kept a steady membership with twenty-eight members.
>
> "The Sulgrave Manor Society in England is named after George Washington's ancestral English home. This Society is relatively small, but active with its seven members.
>
> "The El Camino Real Society in Mexico translates to 'The King's Highway' and was the main line of communication between the old and new country. This Mexico Society has received help and guidance from the Daughters of the American Revolution. With a membership of more than six members, this Society plans to increase membership......"

"The Wayside" in Concord, Massachusetts, where an interpretative guidebook was placed as the National Project

☆ The National President, David A. Smith, and Senior National President, Patricia Love Stephens, were elected and installed.

1994–1996

National President 1994 – 1995	Senior National President 1994 – 1996

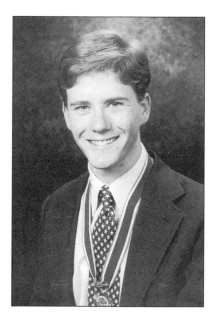 

David A. Smith *Saratoga, California*	**Patricia Love Stephens** *Dallas, Texas*

STARTING OUR CENTENNIAL YEAR

☆ National Theme: FOR PATRIOTS' DREAMS
☆ National Project: Commission a painting of the illustration on our original charter.

Centennial Theme
PRIDE OF THE PAST, PROMISE OF THE FUTURE

For Patriots' Dreams

Centennial Project
Commission a bronze sculpture
of an
American Bald Eagle
as
"A GIFT TO THE NATION"
to be placed at the
National Zoological Park
in Washington, D.C.

☆ On June 6, 1994, the Senior National Board of Management approved the following:

> Production of a minimum of 250 Limited Edition Prints and 1,000 posters from the original art work replicating the illustration on the original charter; Limited editions to be sold for $50.00 each, and posters at $1.00 each plus shipping and handling.
>
> Production of a bronze American Bald Eagle to be placed at an appropriate site—e.g. the National Zoological Park- at a cost not to exceed $50,000.
>
> That a minimum of 200 engraved Jefferson cups be sold for $15.00 each plus shipping and handling.
>
> Advertising of Centennial Pins in five issues of the Daughters of the American Revolution Magazine.
>
> The Administrator to order five new desks and six chairs.
>
> Conservation of militia coat from the War of 1812.

☆ DREAM COMES TRUE FOR PATRIOT

A Soldier's Jacket Lives Again

A militia infantry uniform coat worn in the War of 1812 has received its marching orders in its battle for survival. Smithsonian consultant and noted textile conservator, Virginia Pledger, has been retained by N.S.C.A.R. to research Captain William Reynolds' coat. The C.A.R. Museum currently has on exhibit Captain Reynolds' uniform belt buckle and saber with crested silver eagle head and black leather scabbard with three silver mounts.

☆ Brought back by popular demand. Did you know you can advertise in the *Children of the American Revolution Magazine*? Any member, senior, society, business, or corporation may send black and white, camera ready advertising, and photographs.

☆ SAR NEWSLETTER ENDOWMENT FUND FOR C.A.R.

At the 1994 National SAR Congress, it was announced that because of the continuing generosity of Mrs. Paul M. Niebell, Sr., Honorary Senior National President, N.S.C.A.R., the SAR will grant the Eleanor Smallwood Niebell Award each year to both the State C.A.R. Society and the local C.A.R. Society which have been judged to have the best newsletter by the guidelines set up by The National Society of the Children of the American Revolution.

☆ Society Activities:

Timothy Hatch Society, Madison, Wisconsin, donated seventy children's books to a community center.

New Mexico State Society became a Zoo Parent. It adopted a Mexican Grey Wolf at the Rio Grande Zoo in Albuquerque.

Morven Society, Princeton, New Jersey, is raising funds to buy an 18th Century style medical scale for the hospital room at the Old Barracks Museum.

Members of Little Mountain Society, Painesville, Ohio, as part of their conservation and community service project, spray painted a railway trestle to cover the graffiti.

Cavalier Society, Virginia Beach, Virginia, attended the 74th annual celebration of the first landing of settlers 387 years ago.

Many Societies participate in the Adopt-A-Highway Program in various states, but the Kendall Coles Society, Morristown, New Jersey, was surprised when they were presented a check for $500 by its local township for taking part in the program.

David H. Turner, Sculptor, of Onley, Virginia, shown with his eagle creation for our Gift to the Nation

For its 1994 observance of Constitution Day, the D.C.C.A.R. planted a tree in Rock Creek Cemetery in honor of Abraham Baldwin, the only signer of the Constitution buried in the District of Columbia.

☆ N.S.C.A.R. Peewee Patriots came into being. These are C.A.R. members ten years old and under. They have their own special pages in the *Children of the American Revolution Magazine*. At the Centennial Convention there will be the CAMP C.A.R.: an interactive environment for children under ten years of age and their parents. There will be many planned activities including story hours, music times, special patriotic art projects, movies, and a very special "Happy Birthday C.A.R." party.

☆ On October 17, 1994, the Senior National Board of Management approved the following:

The National Society will discontinue returning supporting data with the duplicate copy of the application; the National Society will continue to return original data to the parents of the applicants, only one original copy of an application be submitted; photocopying will be done after genealogical information has been entered by the genealogist.

The N.S.C.A.R. will submit wording to the Smithsonian Institution to appear on the plaque presented to the National Zoological Park in conjunction with the Eagle Sculpture to appear with the sculpture.

The Centennial Committee will purchase a commemorative souvenir for each attendee of the National Convention at a total cost not to exceed $1,000.

☆ The 1992 C.A.R. National Project—a new Lunchroom Office at Kate Duncan Smith DAR School at Grant, Alabama—was dedicated in October 1994.

☆ On December 5, the Senior National Board of Management, authorized the following:

A minimum of 200 eagle hand puppets be purchased to be sold with profits going to the Centennial Committee

N.S.C.A.R. publish the history of the first one hundred years, seed money to be donated by Mrs. Paul M. Niebell, Sr., profit to go to the Centennial Fund.

☆ The *Daughters of the American Revolution 1995 Annual Calendar* featured C.A.R. in February. A short history and four pictures of members are on the page.

☆ On Monday, January 16, 1995, the members of George Washington, Mount Vernon, and Harriett Lothrop Societies united with friends to honor Elizabeth Prince Bennett Campaigne, C.A.R. National President 1961-1962, a mother who gave two active C.A.R. members, and a current C.A.R. Senior Leader in this C.A.R. Centennial Year.

☆ At the February 6, Senior National Board of Management, approval was given for the following:

The Registrar General of the DAR and SAR, Registrars of State Societies of the S.R. and members of the genealogical staffs of those societies may examine papers when engaged in the verification of applications presented to the societies and that they may photocopy data of open records.

The sale of miniature eagle sculptures at a cost of $400 each, profit to the Centennial Fund.

The Centennial Committee be authorized to spend not more than $200 on a Centennial Exhibit to be displayed at the 1995 National Convention.

The Centennial Committee purchase a minimum of 1,000 Centennial logo note cards to be sold in packages of ten, price not to exceed $10, profit to go to the Centennial Fund.

☆ The March 1995 issue of the *Children of the American Revolution Magazine* had the first paid advertisement.

☆ The Illinois State Society presented a large replica of the N.S.C.A.R. Insignia to the National Society as a Centennial Gift. The Yowani Society, C.A.R., and the Chickasawhy Chapter, DAR, in Waynesboro, Mississippi, donated a huge birthday cake which was displayed at National Convention. Artist, Catherine L. Bohrman of Connecticut presented to the National Society a marble sculpture of a mother Eagle and Eaglet.

☆ On April 20, the Senior National Board of Management approved the following:

William Fairfield Society, Portland, Maine, to use the C.A.R. Insignia on a plaque for the marking of a tree the Society planted in historic Stroudwater Park.

Centennial Logo

The Ohio State Society to use the C.A.R. Insignia on a plaque to be placed at the Rutherford B. Hayes Presidential Center in Fremont, Ohio, with the State Project, a replica of an antique toy train.

Complete revision of the N.S.C.A.R. Bylaws.

In honor of the C.A.R. Centennial, the use of Constitution Hall has been approved by the Executive Committee, NSDAR, for the installation of officers of the Children of the American Revolution on Sunday, April 23, 1995.

☆ Our Senior National President, Patricia Love Stephens, is also DAR National Chairman of the Children of the American Revolution Committee. She gave her report at the NSDAR Continental Congress. After she completed her report, the President General, Mrs. Donald Shattuck Blair, asked that she pause a few moments. They had a surprise for her. She could not imagine what was happening!

The National Chairman of the Resolutions Committee, a good friend of C.A.R., Mrs. Darnell Eggleston, came to the podium. She read a resolution written by the Committee. Mrs. Eggleston then moved that the 104th Continental Congress of the Daughters of the American Revolution pass this Resolution.

The Resolution read as follows:

In Commemoration
of the
100th Birthday
of the
Children of the American Revolution

WHEREAS, On April 5, 1895, during a meeting of the National Board of Management a decision was adopted by the Founders of the National Society Daughters of the American Revolution to incorporate the Children of the American Revolution (C.A.R.) as a separate organization: and

WHEREAS, The C.A.R. adheres to its creed that it is an organization for the training of young people in true patriotism and love of country in order that they shall be better fitted for American citizenship; therefore be it

RESOLVED, The National Society Daughters of the American Revolution applaud the Children of the American Revolution on its 100th Anniversary, recognizing its endeavors to fulfill the objectives of its Society which are as relevant today as in 1895, and it is our pleasure to say HAPPY BIRTHDAY to these future leaders!

This Resolution unanimously passed with a standing ovation!

The President General then afforded Patricia Love Stephens the opportunity to thank the Daughters. She told them how very much the National Society of the Children of the American Revolution, appreciates this surprise Resolution. It also gave her an opportunity to thank the Daughters for the wonderful article in the April 1995 issue of *the Daughters of the American Revolution Magazine*. This article, written by Honorary National President Elizabeth Prince Bennett Campaigne, has wonderful pictures and is in glorious full color.

She further thanked them, on behalf of the National Society, for the wonderful Birthday Gift. The Daughters gave the Children the use of Constitution Hall for the Memorial and Installation Services on Sunday, at no cost, as a Birthday Gift. She thanked them for this very generous present and told them how excited the members are about this opportunity to use this historic and beautiful building.

☆ On opening night of the DAR Continental Congress, the National President and the Senior National President brought greetings to the Daughters. Mrs. Stephens presented a gift to the Daughters, a Miniature Bronze Sculpture of the "Gift to the Nation" from the Children. This miniature sculpture was Number Four, because C.A.R. was founded at the Fourth Continental Congress of DAR.

David Smith presented the Daughters with a framed print #1 of the Limited Edition Print of his National Project. Mrs. Donald Shattuck Blair, President General, NSDAR, accepted print #1 of a limited edition of a painting on the original C.A.R. charter:

☆ On opening night of the Annual Convention, immediately after the Centennial Chairman Elizabeth Lee gave her report, the audience was surprised by the appearance of two real live American Bald Eagles, Challenger and America. Mr. Al Cecere of the National Foundation to Protect America's Eagles, Nashville, Tennessee, brought greetings with the Eagles and explained the goals of the Foundation and how C.A.R. could help. After the session, the eagles were outside the Convention hall on a perch and the children of all ages were fascinated and awed by them.

☆ The Convention had another surprise on Saturday morning. After the report of the National President, David A. Smith, the National Project, the painting on the original charter which was commissioned by the National Society, was unveiled and dedicated. After that session, the participants had a photo opportunity and an opportunity to see the painting up close.

☆ The annual Banquet on Saturday night was a huge Birthday Party to C.A.R. for more than a thousand attendees. The Centennial Logo was on

Mrs. Donald Shattuck Blair, President General, NSDAR, accepting print #1 of a painting on the original C.A.R. Charter, from David A. Smith, National President, N.S.C.A.R.

Mrs. Joseph Wathen, Administrator, shown with Challenger and America, the American Bald Eagles who performed for the Centennial Convention

a huge banner above the head table. Centennial pins were presented to one hundred and eight lucky recipients.

⭐ The Honorary National Presidents who attended the Centennial Convention were:

Elizabeth Bennett Campaigne	Samuel Walton Huddleston, II
Jane Wells Freeny Keegan	Marie Perkins Fridenmaker
Sharon Kay Krueger Lusk	Eric D. Radwick
Philip Field Horne	Donald J. E. Molloy
Rodney H. C. Schmidt	G. Taylor Davis
Michelle B. Loughery Moss	Heather Love Stephens
Charla Borchers Leon	Robert Douglas Warren
Katherine Kennedy Cornwell	Elizabeth Ann Lee

Ten Honorary Senior National Presidents attended:

Mrs. Byron M. Vanderbilt	Mrs. Thomas H. Conner
Mrs. Roy D. Allan	Mrs. Howard R. Kuhn
Mrs. Fred W. Krueger	Mrs. Robert Lorenzo Boggs
Mrs. Stanleigh Swan	Mrs. Howard E. Byrne
Mrs. Thomas G. Burkey	Mrs. Paul M. Niebell, Sr.

⭐ On Sunday, April. 23, 1995, the Centennial Pilgrimage participants arrived at the National Zoological Park for the dedication of the bronze sculpture of an American bald eagle—the "GIFT TO THE NATION"—from the Children and enjoyed a beautiful program.

The program participants were David A. Smith, National President; Laura Jane Jarrell, Incoming National President; Mr. David H. Turner of Turner Sculpture; Elizabeth A. Lee, National Centennial Chairman; Dr. Michael Robinson, Director, National Zoological Park; and Laura H. Lupo, National Chaplain.

Following are the National President's remarks:

Good Morning. We are gathered together this morning to dedicate the Centennial Project of the National Society of the Children of the American Revolution, the oldest patriotic youth organization in the United States.

"A Gift to the Nation," a bronze American Bald Eagle sculpture, commissioned by the Children of the American Revolution, has been executed by Mr. David Turner of Turner Sculpture, Onley, Virginia. The sculpture commemorates the 100th Anniversary of the founding of the Children of the American Revolution in April, 1895.

The eagle, a patriotic symbol of pride and promise soars over the earth in its quest for freedom. It indeed symbolizes and permeates the Pride of the Past — and Promise of the Future, the Centennial Theme of the Children of the American Revolution.

Today marks an historical time in C.A.R.'s existence. May the pride of the past, these first one hundred years, truly be the promise of the future, only the beginning of what is yet to come.

Elizabeth A. Lee, National Centennial Chairman of the Children of the American Revolution, will present the Centennial Project. Mr. Turner and Dr. Robinson will join her while the National President and Incoming National President unveil the Eagle.

The acceptance of the Eagle will be made by Dr. Robinson.

The plaque for A Gift To The Nation was mounted at the base of the eagle sculpture.

Other distinguished guests present were: Patricia Love Stephens, Senior National President, National Society of the Children of the American Revolution; Marie Perkins Fridenmaker, Senior National Chaplain and Senior Centennial Chairman, National Society of the Children of the American Revolution; Dr. Robert Hoage, Chief, Office of Public Affairs, The National Zoological Park, Smithsonian Institution and

The American Bald Eagle plaque presented to the National Zoological Park in Washington, D.C., located in front of our Gift to the Nation

The American Bald Eagle sculpture with Patricia Love Stephens, Senior National President (1994-1996); David A. Smith, National President (1994-1995); and Laura Jane Jarrell, National President (1995-1996). Picture taken by Mr. Scott C. Shewmaker, Senior State President, D.C.C.A.R.

Mrs. Beverly Turner, wife of Mr. David Turner, and their three children, Jason, Rachel and Rebecca.

National Chaplain, Laura H. Lupo, offered the closing prayer.

The National President then said that the permanent home of the American Bald Eagle Sculpture will be at the Bald Eagle Exhibit here at the National Zoological Park.

☆ EVENTS AT DAR CONSTITUTION HALL

David A. Smith, National President, placed a wreath at the DAR Founders Memorial Monument in memory of our beloved Founder, Harriett Mulford Lothrop. He said that her dreams for this organization have survived for one hundred years and we hereby pledge to continue those dreams into the future.

A Panoramic Photograph of all the attendees with the C.A.R. Centennial Logo Banner, was taken on the steps of DAR Constitution Hall.

The National and Senior National Officers processed into the Hall and experienced the majestic and awe-inspiring appearance of the Flag of the United States of America as it dropped from the ceiling over the head of the National President.

The program began when the National President opened the meeting and thanked everyone for being at this exciting and momentous occasion. He invited Mr. David Turner to bring greetings. Elizabeth Lee, National Centennial Chairman, then asked the National Presidents, incoming and outgoing, the Senior National President and Mr. Turner to come to the center aisle at the base of the stage for the presentation of the miniature Eagles and a photo opportunity. Eagle #1 was presented to Mrs. Glenn Johnson. A big "Thank You" was given to Mrs. Johnson. The Eagle Project was her idea—now a dream come true.

Following the Memorial Service and Installation Ceremony, the National President said:

> Each of you has been here in attendance at this momentous time in the history of our wonderful organization. C.A.R. has touched the lives of all of us. We have made wonderful friends. We have continued to accomplish the dreams of our founder, Harriett Mulford Lothrop, and perpetuate the dreams of our Patriots. As we go forward into the next century, we must continue this important work. We must

Mr. David H. Turner of Turner Sculpture and Mrs. Glenn Johnson, Senior National Librarian-Curator, with #1 of the Miniature Eagles presented during the N.S.C.A.R. 1995 Annual Pilgrimage

continue to perpetuate the dreams of our founder. We must also be prepared to teach future generations the principles of our founding fathers. They are the Pride of our Past, but we are the Promise of our Future. Everyone please stand and join hands for the singing of God Bless America, thus ending the 100th National Centennial Convention."

An extra special presentation then took place. All of a sudden Constitution Hall was lighted by only one candle on the stage. From the shadows, a man, dressed in Colonial costume, appeared in the light of that candle. He described the events leading up to the signing of the *Declaration of Independence*. He told what a monumental decision it was. It meant war, the American Revolution, it meant that if they lost that war, it was an act of treason, for which hanging was the punishment. It meant the loss of everything held dear, home, family, fortune and life. But he had made his decision. He would sign his name to the Declaration of Independence. He then challenged all who wished to do the same, to come forward and sign their name. The signers got to take their own signed copy of the *Declaration of Independence* home with them as a memento of this occasion.

In addition to all of the C.A.R. members, seniors, friends and relatives, the newly installed DAR National Officers, Mrs. Charles Keil Kemper and her associates, also attended.

☆ At the Tomb of the Unknown Soldier of the American Revolution, Amber Thompson, of Oklahoma, played taps at the service which was conducted by Rachel Anne Alarid, National Chairman, and Mrs. Gordon W. Keegan, Jr.,[5] Senior National Chairman. A wreath was placed by Rhiana Graham, State President of New Mexico.

This was followed by a ceremony at Mt. Vernon at the Tomb of George and Martha Washington.

☆ Miss Laura Jane Jarrell was installed as the incoming National President.

---

[5]Mrs. Keegan was Jane Wells Freeny, National President 1967-68.

National President
1995 – 1996

Laura Jane Jarrell
Vienna, Virginia

ON TO CENTENNIAL PLUS ONE

☆ National Theme: C.A.R.—THE DAWN OF A NEW DAY

☆ National Project: Raise funds to Adopt, Name and Release into its natural habitat a baby American Bald Eagle.

☆ On June 5, 1995, the Senior National Board of Management approved the following:

Purchase of a backup computer storage device and disk cartridges.

Senior National Librarian-Curator to retain the professional services of a textile conservator to conserve the dress of Harriett M. Lothrop, the hand-sewn thirteen-star American flag made in Connecticut during the American Revolution, and the child's cap made by Martha Washington for her granddaughter.

Senior National Librarian-Curator to retain services to render a condition report on the painting of Harriett M. Lothrop dedicated April 20, 1915.

C.A.R. - THE DAWN OF A NEW DAY
National Theme Button

Senior National Librarian-Curator to order acid-free archival materials.

Senior National Librarian-Curator to engage services to construct a model of an American Revolutionary time-period sailing vessel.

Senior National President to contact Gadsby's Tavern regarding items on loan from N.S.C.A.R.

Painting of N.S.C.A.R. Museum walls and ceiling.

Display of a Centennial Exhibit in the N.S.C.A.R. Museum.

Printing of the newly revised edition of the N.S.C.A.R. Bylaws.

Purchase of additional file cabinets and one fire-retardant file cabinet.

Purchase or lease or lease-to-purchase a copy machine.

Establish The Eleanor Smallwood Niebell Endowment Fund.

Pennsylvania State Society to imprint the C.A.R. Centennial Insignia on backpacks and tote bags, profit to go to the N.S.C.A.R. Centennial Fund.

Illinois State Society use the C.A.R. Insignia, the C.A.R. Centennial Insignia on a banner and the C.A.R. wooden Insignia in a parade for community activities.

D.C. State Society use the C.A.R. Centennial Insignia on luggage tags, profit to the N.S.C.A.R. Centennial Fund.

☆ Society Activities:

San Jacinto Society, Houston, Texas, adopted an Attwater Prairie Chicken at the Houston Zoo.

Members of the George Wythe Society, Williamsburg, Virginia, placed baskets at a local marina to collect aluminum cans for a recycling project.

Missouri State Society has an Investor's Fund which helps members attend National Convention.

The Battle of Thomas Creek Society, Winter Park, Florida, participated in Veterans Day activities in Orlando where a vintage World War II aircraft flew over, concluding the ceremonies.

Montana State Society announced the Miss Marjorie Stevenson C.A.R. Scholarship. Sponsored by Montana State Society and Friends of Miss Stevenson.

☆ On June 19, at the NSSAR Congress in Louisville, Kentucky, the first winner of the NSSAR Eleanor Smallwood Niebell Award for the Best Local Society C.A.R. Newsletter was awarded to Old Stage Road Society, Memphis, Tennessee. The Louisiana State Society won the State Society Award.

☆ In July 1995, *Good Morning America*, a popular morning news program by ABC (American Broadcasting Company), aired some of the National Officers of C.A.R. saying "Good morning, America." The program also announced that the National Society of the Children of the American Revolution had just celebrated its 100th Birthday.

☆ On October 16, the Senior National Board of Management approved the following:

Establish a policy that all N.S.C.A.R. public domain printed material be permitted to appear in multi-media communications.

N.S.C.A.R. Museum cases be varnished, stained at a cost not to exceed $600.

*Mrs. Paul M. Niebell, Sr., Honorary Senior National President, N.S.C.A.R.;
Jonathan W. Smith, National Vice President for Mid-Southern Region,
N.S.C.A.R.; receiving the award for his society, Colonel Stewart B. McCarty,
Jr., President General, NSSAR; Laura Jane Jarrell, National President,
N.S.C.A.R.; and Patricia Love Stephens, Senior National President, N.S.C.A.R.*

An additional $285 be paid for the lamination of the N.S.C.A.R. Centennial exhibit, money to come from the Centennial Fund.

Accepted with thanks and gratitude the Video Library Centennial Gift presented to the National Society by Patricia Love Stephens, Senior National President, during this Centennial Year.

☆ In October the South Carolina C.A.R. Society dedicated the brick pathway to the Old Tamassee Post Office. "Landscaping the Path for Tomorrow" was a S.C.S.C.A.R. State Project completed in one year. The proceeds were given to the Children's Fund at Tamassee. The path has 255 bricks in honor and memory of friends of Tamassee.

☆ The South Carolina DAR District V honored with pride the South Carolina C.A.R. Society with a picture in the *Daughters of the American Revolution Magazine* showing the Old Tamassee Post Office.

Brick pathway leading to the Old Tamassee Post Office on the campus of the school

Mrs. S. Perry Davis, Senior State President, S.C.S.C.A.R., Calvin Cook, Honorary State President, S.C.S.C.A.R., and National Chairman Patriotic Symbols, N.S.C.A.R.; and Mrs. Drake Harden Rogers, Past Vice President for Southeastern Region, N.S.C.A.R.; in front of the Old Tamassee Post Office

☆ The December 4 Senior National Board of Management approved the following:

Accept with appreciation the gift of the "Official Spoon of the N.S.C.A.R." made by John Lamar Kimbell, Jr., a then member of the John Hancock Society, Shreveport, Louisiana. The gift is in memory of Louise Monsell Bennett and given by her daughter, Elizabeth Bennett Campaigne; son, Timothy R. Bennett; and grandchildren David and Christina Campaigne, credit to the Mount Vernon Society, D.C.C.A.R. The spoon was made circa 1913 and was sold through Galt & Brothers, Washington, D.C.

The cost over-run of $345.65 for paint and labor for painting the C.A.R. Museum.

☆ Lindsay Ames, President of the Oklahoma State Society, presented C.A.R. miniature eagle #168 to the Oklahoma City Zoo in memory of the victims of the bombing at the Alfred P. Murrah Federal Building, April, 1995.

☆ The Senior National Board approved the following on February 5, 1996:

Expenditures at the Tomb of the Unknown Soldier of the American Revolution to paint the fence not to exceed $500; to purchase a display case and stand, cost not to exceed $1,000, and a digital recorder, amplification system with necessary rewiring, not to exceed $1,200 at the Tomb.

That Mrs. Paul M. Niebell, Sr., Honorary Senior National President, use the C.A.R. Centennial Logo on the cover of the hardbound Centennial Book to be published.

That all documents pertaining to the NSDAR proposal for C.A.R. space be sent to the National and Senior National Board Members and Chairmen.

☆ On April 18, the Senior National Board of Management adopted the following:

To accession the museum quality model of the sloop Providence constructed by Colan D. Ratliff, Marine architect and ship model builder and to attach a brief history of the Providence to the accession report.

Established a Sesquicentennial Fund with a beginning balance of $1,995 to be taken from the Centennial Fund.

That all contracts, except those involving National Convention, must be presented to the Senior National Board of Management for review for acceptance or rejection.

Establish a standing committee to be known as the C.A.R.-DAR-SAR-S.R. Relations Committee to foster increased interaction among the four Societies.

☆ The second year winners of the NSSAR Eleanor Smallwood Niebell Award for the Best Local Society C.A.R. Newsletter went again to Old Stage Road Society, Memphis, Tennessee, and the Michigan State Society won the State Society Award.

☆ At the 101st Annual Convention, immediately after the National President's report, Laura Jane Jarrell presented Mr. Al Cecere a check for $5,000 for the National Foundation to Protect America's Eagles. *Freedom Flyer* was the name the members voted for their bird.

On August 12, 1996, at 7:00 P.M., *Freedom Flyer* flew. The 1995-1996 National Project was completed. *Freedom Flyer* represents the freedom courage, and strength of eagles. Yet, it is that same freedom, courage, and strength that our forefathers valued, and that we as members of the C.A.R. continue to value.

Freedom Flyer and friend, at twelve weeks old, getting ready to be released from the hack tower near Dollywood, Tennessee

Final Thoughts About the Centennial Celebration

NEW CENTURY CELEBRATION WHAT WAS IT ALL ABOUT?

by
Mrs. Charla Borchers Leon[6]
Senior Special Events Chairman
1994–1996

What was it all about anyway? Pride and promise, past and future—and belief in it all!

Can you believe it? C.A.R. has been around 101 years and has completed its Centennial Observance with a New Century Celebration!

As you know, the National Society commissioned a life-size bronze American Bald Eagle Sculpture to be presented as "A Gift to the Nation, From the Children." The decision to proceed with the project was one met with cautious speculation, but overwhelming anticipation. Belief in the project made it a reality when in April 1995 the American Bald Eagle

[6]National President 1979-80. This article was originally published in the June 1996 issue of the *Children of the American Revolution Magazine*.

Sculpture was dedicated at the National Zoological Park in Washington, D.C., as a symbol of C.A.R.'s permanent belief of freedom in this country. Two real American Bald Eagles, "Challenger" and "America," awed the young and young-at-heart at the evening business session of the Centennial Convention in 1995 ... and the National Society believed in perpetuating our country's symbol of freedom so strongly that the next year's National Project funds were dedicated to adopting and placing in its own natural habitat a new-born American Bald Eagle. "Challenger" returned to this year's National Convention and soared over the crowd to the podium like only an eagle can. Perhaps that is what enlightened attendees to select by ballot the name "Freedom Flyer" for the new-born American Bald Eagle adopted by C.A.R.!

"Pride of the Past—Promise of the Future" encompassed the room at this year's New Century Celebration Banquet. Centennial National Officers processed to music with spotlights from both corners of the Banquet Hall crossing a festive center platform in the middle of the room flowing to the head table.

The National Society displayed its pride in the past as well as its promise for the future with a dedication of its own time capsule. The contents of the capsule—which in fifty years will be a part of its past—were dramatically secured for the future until the National Society's Sesquicentennial. The plaque for the time capsule reads:

Centennial Time Capsule
dedicated April 20, 1996
National Society
of the
Children of the American Revolution
April 5, 1895—April 5, 1995
celebrating
Pride of the Past—Promise of the Future

This time capsule contains remembrances of the Centennial Celebration and is to be opened during the celebration of the sesquicentennial of the Society in the year 2045.

There is such belief in the future that the National Society set aside $1995 to grow toward that milestone in its history!

Pride in ownership and preservation of the past orchestrated C.A.R.'s Centennial Parade of Artifacts. Museum artifacts which date back through our country's history and profoundly exemplify a proud past were "on parade" at this year's banquet. The National Society believed strongly enough in preserving these prized possessions for a museum rededication. Could you believe it? Because of circumstances beyond the control of C.A.R., it was not possible to visit the C.A.R. Museum at C.A.R. National Headquarters for a rededication ceremony during the Annual Pilgrimage, so the items were brought to the New Century Celebration Banquet for presentation!

With a decade by decade narration of C.A.R.'s past century, artifacts including a bonnet made by Martha Washington for her granddaughter; a replica of the *Providence*, the first sailing vessel of the Continental Navy; a collection of handwork samplers as well as of baby caps; a military jacket from the War of 1812; and a rare American Flag circa 1820—1840 believed to have been flown aboard a sailing ship were showcased through the audience to and from the spotlighted center platform. One-by-one our own young men, each in a tuxedo and special handling gloves, showed our precious possessions to those in attendance. Larger than life, the framed portrait of our founder, Mrs. Harriett M. Lothrop, was rolled in for spotlighted display. Painted by famous American artist, Edmund Tarbell, it stood over eight feet tall and majestically served as the foremost symbol of our past. The audience was summoned to look very carefully at the painting, and as it was described, the very dress in which Mrs. Lothrop was attired in the painting, was brought in on a manikin in a display case. The audience swelled with pride and gave a standing ovation at this display of the Pride of the Past Preserved for the Future.

Peewee Patriots joined National President, Laura Jarrell, for a brief revolutionary story time at the center platform in the Banquet Hall.

When it was all said and done, the new century National Officers and Senior National Officers were introduced jointly and processed to the platform in the center of the room where, hand in hand, they met to begin their tenure of office for the future. Belief in the past as well as what's in store for the future was what the New Century Celebration Convention was all about.

The Sunday Pilgrimage of National Convention was just what the words define. Members and Seniors traveled back in time on a pilgrimage of reflection in honor of patriots who served our country. As the participants stood at the base of the Iwo Jima Memorial, they traveled back half a century to World War II and listened to a current United States Marine tell about the significance of Iwo Jima as well as the history of the monument. The brave patriots who fought to raise that American Flag were saluted with the Pledge of Allegiance and a wreath was laid in their honor. After all, that's what patriotism and love of country was-and is-all about.

The Changing of the Guard and placing of a wreath at the Tomb of the Unknown Soldier at Arlington National Cemetery was a strong, yet meaningful, reminder of the ultimate sacrifice made by many Americans whose duty it has been throughout our history to serve our country. The National Society revisited this awesome site this year as a return to one of C.A.R.'s longstanding traditions. Belief in those whose graves are marked by white head stones on hill after hill instilled reverence from our own. After all, for those who respectfully are laid to rest at Arlington National Cemetery, that is what service to country was supremely about.

The pilgrimage traversed further back in time for the remainder of the day. Wreaths were laid in tribute to our country's founding father, George Washington, and his bride, Martha Washington, at the site of their tomb at Mount Vernon. With a return to tradition once again, installation of National and Senior National Officers was held on the green at Mount Vernon. Seeing is believing—and from the estate grounds entered President George Washington himself who installed the new National President, David Andrew Campaigne[7] and the Senior National President, Mrs. Herbert M. Floyd. He charged them with the presidential duty of leadership. He equally instilled the duty of citizenship to the crowd in attendance. Upon conclusion of the ceremony, President Washington visited with the citizens of the land at his estate and escorted the group to his home for viewing. After all, belief and imagination of the possible is what it is all about!

After a picnic with President Washington at Fort Hunt Park, which is down the road from Mount Vernon and used to be part of one of Mr. Washington's nearby farms, pilgrimage participants heard a brief history of the significance of Fort Hunt during World War II as related by a United States Park Ranger. The group then continued on to yet another traditional location for the Sunday Pilgrimage.

A Memorial Service was conducted at the Old Presbyterian Meeting House in Alexandria, Virginia, remembering our own loved ones gone to a far better life and place since the year before. Let there be Peace on Earth was the mood of the service on reflection on duty, honor, and country. Modern day documentaries were presented by two members, one male and the other a female, the characters whose names were not important but whose deeds in time of war were paramount. One of C.A.R.'s own members, a United States Marine, then conducted an Armed Forces medley salute asking all in the audience who either served or had a relative who served in each respective branch of the military to stand as their military branch song was heard. At the conclusion, this country's first great military leader, General George Washington, entered the room. He militarily

[7]Son of Elizabeth Prince Bennett Campaigne, National President 1961-62.

handed off his sword which was presented to the National Chaplain and incoming National President, David Campaigne, for safe keeping while the General was in the house of worship. General Washington shared with the group the events and circumstances during the winter at Valley Forge and described what our patriot soldiers experienced in the War for Independence. After a few moments of silent prayer, *The Kid Has Gone to the Colors* was heard from the sanctuary's balcony. This poem had been printed in the *Children of the American Revolution Magazine* during World War I.

THE KID HAS GONE TO THE COLORS

The Kid has gone to the Colors
And we don't know what to say;
The Kid we have loved and cuddled
Stepped out for the Flag today
We thought him a child, a baby,
With never a care at all,
But his country called him man-size
And the Kid has heard the call.

He paused to watch the recruiting
Where, fired by fife and drum,
He bowed his head to Old Glory
And thought that it whispered;
"Come!"
The Kid, not being a slacker,
Stood forth with patriot-joy.
To add his name to the roster
And God, we're proud of the boy!

The Kid has gone to the Colors;
It seems but a little while
Since he drilled a schoolboy army
In a truly martial style.
But now he's a man, a soldier.
And we lend him a listening ear.
For his heart is a heart all loyal
Unscourged by the curse of fear.

His dad, when he told him, shuddered,
His mother — God bless her! — cried;
Yet, blest with a mother-nature

237

She wept with a mother-pride.
But he, whose old, shoulders straightened
Was granddad, for memory ran
To years when he, too, a youngster
Was changed by the flag to a man!

W. N. Herschel, *The Indianapolis News*

General Washington's sword was returned to him before the recession to the churchyard where respect was paid to that Unknown Soldier of the American Revolution. After all, that's truly what duty, honor and country was all about!

In the churchyard, Pride of the Past was eloquently relayed in the service at the Tomb of the Unknown Soldier of the American Revolution. The Tomb's history was given, and for the Promise of the Future, a rededication of the Tomb was performed. C.A.R. was responsible for providing for the cleaning of the Tomb, the painting of the fence around it, and providing for the new digital sound system and recorded message as well as an inscribed plaque. As a wreath was placed in memory of the unknown soldier, General Washington came forth and singly saluted his troop. Taps was played. A folded United States Flag was placed on the Tomb by our current day uniformed member of the military.

In reflection of the day's travels from the World War II vintage at Iwo Jima to the resting place of many veterans at Arlington National Cemetery—to the time of our own organization's roots at Mount Vernon and in the churchyard where a soldier is laid to rest—belief in this country, in its past, and for its future, was reverently displayed. The pilgrimage had come full circle; that truly is what C.A.R. is all about!

APPENDIX A

Several well-known persons who were members of the C.A.R.:

General Henry Hawley "HAP" Arnold
Army Air Force

Mrs. George U. Baylies
President General, NSDAR

Elizabeth Dole
President, American Red Cross

Mr. John Foster Dulles
U. S. Secretary of State

Mr. John W. Finger
President General, NSSAR

Mrs. Charles Carroll Haig
National President, N.S.C.A.R.

The Honorable Brereton C. Jones
Governor of Kentucky

Chief Justice Alfred Paul Murrah, Jr.
Chief Justice to the 10th U. S. Circuit Court of Appeals,
Oklahoma City, Oklahoma
(The Oklahoma City Building named for him was the scene
of the 1995 bombing.)

Miss Janet Reno
Attorney General of the United States of America

The Honorable Charles E. Roemer, III
Governor of Louisiana

Mrs. Richard D. Shelby
President General, NSDAR

Miss Margaret Truman
Daughter of Harry S. Truman
President of the United States

APPENDIX B

Some awards and honors received by members of the Children of the American Revolution are:

Boy Scout—God & Country Award

Citation from President Reagan for Outstanding Excellence
in Scholastic Achievement

Dean's List

Eagle Scout Award

4-H Grand Champions

Girl Scout Gold Award

Governor's Award in Conservation

Honored by the Optimist Club
Youth Appreciation Week

Junior American Citizen's National Contest Winner

Kiwanis International Student Achievement Award

National Hiatt Foundation Award

National Honor Society

National Junior Horticulture Association Winner

National Science for Youth Foundation Award

Oratorical Contest Winner

Outstanding Musicianship Award
University of Connecticut Jazz Festival

Outstanding Young Women in America

People to People
Student Ambassadors

Presidential Academic Fitness Award

Recipients of:
DAR American History Essay Contest
DAR Arthur and Lillian Dunn Scholarship
DAR Good Citizen Award

Bronze Congressional Award
Silver Congressional Award
National Merit Scholarship
Westinghouse Family Scholarship

Rotary International Exchange Student

SAR Essay Contest Winner

State Ambassador
to the
Hugh O'Brien Youth Foundation
World Leadership Congress

The American Legion School Award

The Daughters of
Founders and Patriots of America Award

U. S. Achievement Academy National Award

U. S. Army ROTC Nursing Scholarship Award

Who's Who Among American High School Students

Who's Who in American Colleges and Universities

Who's Who in U. S. Mathematics

YMCA Youth Governor

Young Author's Festival Contest Winner

Young Columbus Essay Contest Winner

APPENDIX C

Endowment Fund
$100.00

Museum Renovation Fund
Red Apple
$1,000.00

N.S.C.A.R. Magazine Fund
No longer available

Magazine Fund
$100.00

Magazine Donor Fund
Benjamin Franklin Medallion
$1000.00

Centennial Pins
$100.00 $200.00
                          With diamond

INDEX

247